THE SHIELD OF ACHILLES

By Horace Gregory

Poems

CHELSEA ROOMING HOUSE

NO RETREAT

A WREATH FOR MARGERY

CHORUS FOR SURVIVAL

POEMS 1930-1940

Translation

THE POEMS OF CATULLUS

Criticism

PILGRIM OF THE APOCALYPSE:
A critical study of D. H. Lawrence

Editor

NEW LETTERS IN AMERICA

THE TRIUMPH OF LIFE

HORACE GREGORY

The Shield of Achilles

Essays on Beliefs in Poetry

HARCOURT, BRACE AND COMPANY, NEW YORK

A WARTIME BOOK

*This complete edition is produced in full
compliance with the government's regu-
lations for conserving paper and other
essential materials.*

A FOREWORD WITH ACKNOWLEDGMENTS

AT the risk of oversimplifying my intentions, and that risk lies open to everyone who writes a foreword to a book of essays in criticism, I offer an explanation for this book's title. At this point there is always much to be said in favor of saying nothing at all, of allowing the reader to find out for himself whatever the title may mean or hope to mean in the mind of the person who wrote the book. I am also aware that to explain the title of a book of this kind is to point a moral—but I have already decided to take my chances of seeming to stress a moral attitude in regard to literature, and there is certainly no advantage in trying to disregard the truth of my position. How then does *The Shield of Achilles* apply to the writers I have elected to talk about in the fifteen essays of this book? And what does *The Shield of Achilles* mean?

Since the shield has been best described by Homer, and since there is always a proper ambiguity in poetry, one should not be too ruthlessly dogmatic in speaking of its meaning. But we do know that the shield was Vulcan's work and, perhaps, his masterpiece, and we have long accepted Homer's authority in respect to that knowledge. There is no particular mystery about the shield itself: it was given to Achilles, and it was made to be useful as well as beautiful; and there is nothing obscure about the use that Achilles made of it. The true question arises when we consider the care with which Homer described it; it is then that we begin to perceive the many images, or rather, the many reflections of life that the shield carried on its surface: there one looks upward to huge Orion and the Bear, and below them to the scenes of war and peace on earth. The description is such (and I believe I am not the first to remark upon it) that we are inclined to see in its creation an analogy to and a criterion for the art of writing poetry. Perhaps the story of the shield was in fact the statement— as far as he cared to make it—of Homer's esthetic, leaving his critics to interpret it, or to answer it, as best they could. However that may be, the story of the shield remains a valid criterion for poetry in any age; and today, its associations of war in respect to human activity seem less inappropriate than they did, let us say, some fifty years ago. In saying this, I wish to make it clear that I do not believe that art is a weapon, but I do believe that a weapon, if it is finely tempered and accurate, can resemble in the seriousness of its purpose a work of art.

Nearly a dozen of the essays that I have assembled here are concerned with poetry and the lives of men who wrote it, and therefore, the image of Achilles' shield concerns the subject of my book. It might be said that all the writers of whom I speak created with variable success an Achilles' shield with which to face the world. This is true enough, but the shield, if it is to have any meaning at all, must apply more directly to the writing of poetry, and must be less than all-embracing in its definition.

Among the essays I have included in this book, there is one that refers to a discussion of poetry that took place between Lewis Carroll's Alice and her White Knight. Perhaps the discussion lacked the serious overtones that many people associate with a conversation of that kind, but for my purpose the atmosphere was eminently correct; the conversation went to the root of the matter whenever it touched upon the many names that any particular poem might be called; and in recollecting it, I suggested that the shield of Achilles may be taken to mean the degree of self-knowledge that a work of art contains to protect itself against what has been so often called "the ravages of time." The shield then seems to protect the author of a poem, reviving his name even from the deepest obscurity, and offering through its example a protection for the reader. There is little doubt that Achilles' shield dazzled and disarmed his enemies; and if the shield may be said to contain a moral purpose in its creation, it was rather more than artfully concealed within the arts of persuasion that it employed.

I must confess that I have a great interest in morality as a humane art, and for that reason I have opened my book with a reconsideration of the poems of Samuel Johnson, and closed it with a tribute to the *Shelburne Essays* of Paul Elmer More. Morality, I fear, is not to be found among the liberal arts, and therefore its presence may seem to wear a stern face to those who believe that to know all is to forgive everything that happens in a sometimes well-intentioned, but surely less than perfect, world.

As for the shield of Achilles, others may well endow it with meanings that do not coincide with mine. But I also think that many will agree (and this is true of all great works of art) that a variety of interpretations cannot destroy it; they may, at times, misrepresent it, but if they are sufficiently sustained over lengthening periods of time, they are a test and, finally, a proof of its vitality.

A number of the essays I have selected for republication in this book owe the sources of their being to the following list of periodicals. Several have been enlarged and completely rewritten after their appearance in the *Herald Tribune* Books, the *Nation*, the *New Republic*, and the

Saturday Review of Literature; and one appeared in the New York *Times* Book Review in very nearly the same form that it is now presented to the reader. Others have been reshaped (and in most instances contracted slightly) to fall within the scope of the present volume after their publication in the *Southern Review,* the *Atlantic Monthly,* the *Partisan Review* and *Signatures.* The essay on Alice and her White Knight and Wordsworth's *Ode* on Immortality was spoken as a lecture at Columbia University in the City of New York before the English Institute during the first week of September in 1941. The note on D. H. Lawrence and his posthumous reputation was among the pieces included in Mr. Morton D. Zabel's *Literary Opinion in America* (Harper & Bros.), 1937. My remarks on Dr. William Carlos Williams were first published as an introduction to a new edition of his book *In the American Grain* (New Directions), 1939. In all these instances I wish to thank the editors of the publications in which these pieces first saw light. I also wish to thank Mr. Theodore Spencer of Harvard University for a helpful criticism of my essay on W. B. Yeats.

H. G.

Palisades, New York
October 4th, 1943

CONTENTS

xii

THE SHIELD OF ACHILLES

ON SAMUEL JOHNSON IN THE TWENTIETH
CENTURY

A NEW edition of Samuel Johnson's *Poems* * is on the library table, its pages freshly cut, its magnificent type-face visible to all who enjoy the reading of a well-printed and sensibly bound book. The book is a luxury, for its price is seven dollars and fifty cents, and being what it is, a book of poems, and many of them in Latin, it is quite impossible to think of it being loaned from the stationery shop, "Where fiction flourishes," one almost says, "and arts decay." The book has been the patient, brilliant, cautious labor of almost twenty years in research by two editors, a work of collaboration which bridged the Atlantic westward, using the resources of the Huntington and Yale libraries, and publishing for the first time in a complete collection of Johnson's verse some half a hundred pieces, including translations into English of the Latin and Greek mottoes and quotations in *The Rambler*. The result is, I repeat, a beautiful book—and a luxury—and I am reminded, perhaps irreverently, of the protest that Samuel Johnson wrote to the printers at Oxford concerning the high prices of their fine books. That was almost two hundred years ago, and I am reassured that human nature as well as its learning process, even in universities, may change with

---

* *The Poems of Samuel Johnson*, edited by David Nichol Smith and Edward L. McAdam. Oxford at The Clarendon Press: 1941. $7.50.

time for better or for worse, but the progress, whenever it moves, is very, very slow.

As one turns the pages of Johnson's *Poems* in their new dress, many questions are opened to the mind, and the first of these is a test of our general interest in the eighteenth century. Why is Johnson's verse revived today, and why is it that both his verse and prose awaken respect as well as curiosity? Two generations ago quotations from Boswell's *Life of Johnson* occasioned more amusement than enjoyment or a serious regard, and the occasion (inspired perhaps by readings of Macaulay, Thackeray, and Taine) was a signal for hilarity rather than respect. But to continue with our question: Is the revival of Johnson a mere turning of the wheel that raises the fame of one writer and his age and obscures the others, a recurrent movement accompanied by the cries of "Down with Shelley, up with Pope; it is growing far too late for Donne and Crashaw, therefore, up with Johnson—and do not forget that excellent though neglected poet, Christopher Smart"? Is our interest in Johnson's major writings, his "Lives" of Milton, Savage, and Pope, *The Vanity of Human Wishes* and his *London* a subconscious desire to unsay Wordsworth's *Preface* to the second edition of the *Lyrical Ballads?*—that preface which was written in the wraith-like but resounding presence of Johnson's authority and which dispelled that shadow for an hundred years to come? I think not. Nor is our general curiosity concerning an age that was devout, and yet followed the lights of reason, a complete rejection of all nineteenth century notions of progress in the worship of scientific skills and innovations. This general question, no matter how briefly answered, and in which I may have seemed to persist at length, supplies a key and perhaps unlocks a door to a few of the multiple reasons why Johnson's stature has not decreased during a

4

generation that has felt the earth shake with the impact of two world wars. In times such as our own, all serious writing reflects the strength of radical conviction (and Johnson was decidedly radical in his expression of conservative beliefs), all scenes that mirror the origin of our institutions as they are today attain the power and vividness of a renewed perception into the heart of human activity. In England—and I am thinking of the island and not the near and far reaches of the British Empire—the appeal of an eighteenth century formality in literary diction, wit, and manner has its own elegiac, and one might say, "romantic" air. It is of the same heightened mood that a young man or woman achieves in a last look about the house before leaving home for foreign lands; the look embraces all things with an unconscious lift of being: chairs, tables, doors, and windows take on the quality of animate life and seem to speak; and for the first time, each in its proper place acquires meanings that hitherto had been left in darkness, and until this moment had been unfelt, unknown. Something of that sensibility, which one hesitates to call "emotion," has been conveyed by Edith Sitwell's book on Bath and in her *Alexander Pope;* and one finds that in her literary essays Virginia Woolf is at her happiest when she brings to mind Dr. Burney's evening parties in Poland Street, or the masks that Horace Walpole wore to face the world. These are tributes written to a past which has an imaginative being within the present, but is perceived in years of crisis as though it were seen for the last time. On our side of the Atlantic—and may we take it as a symbol that the senior editor of Johnson's *Poems* is David Nichol Smith and that his collaborator, Mr. McAdam, is an American?—on our side of the water, the memory of eighteenth century imagination and its initiative revives the day that saw the birth of our governmental institutions;

5

and remembering them, we accept the contradictions of our national heroes, Washington, Adams, Hamilton, Marshall, and Jefferson, as a peculiarly American complex whose continuity remains unbroken and today reasserts its claim to an enduring life.

We can then agree, I think, that with all the visible changes which have taken place in the last two hundred years, differences in dress, in architecture, in social habits, in modes of speech and of travel, our general outlook toward the eighteenth century is neither disinterested, nor unreasonably cold. But in speaking of so broad a view and looking into the new edition of Johnson's *Poems*, another question rises: What of Johnson's view, how far did it go, was it clear or clouded; did it run farther than that queer distance he described "from China to Peru," by air or land or sea, and did it in a final glance embrace the world? That is a pertinent question in a day when world-views are extremely popular and the names of many places ring in our ears. We wait for news from foreign correspondents, we rely on photographs of distant towns and cities, and some of us have perfected the art of tuning in casually on short-wave length cycles of the bright-dialed radio; the view is globular and swift, but not, I fear, completely translatable to sight and feeling on the written page. In articles and even in books of considerable bulk written by experts, so I have heard, of world affairs, the *Weltanschauung* grows thin with the blue of empyrean distances: whole nations, plateaus, valleys, mountain ranges, and even continents are bombed off the earth, replanned, and perhaps repopulated within a single paragraph; the world-view, since we must have it, is still there, but its skirts (if I may change the figure) are of sheerest organdy, and the lady looks shameless, anemic, and about to perish in a winter storm. A world-view of this sort, I must confess, does not

6

appear in Johnson's prose or verse, nor does a world-view of another kind, and of a sort expressed by the deliberate philosopher, a Thomas Hobbes, a Bishop Berkeley, or a Professor Whitehead, enter the central stream of Johnson's morality. Despite the strength of Johnson's will and mind, it would be possible to argue that he was not an intellectual at all, and if we insist upon reading a world-view into the content of Johnson's verse we must speak in terms of a theology nourished by the Anglican Church, and then agree that it was of a different order than that which possessed the imagination of his peers.

It is of some significance to know that in conversation Johnson's vowels were spoken with the same accent which marked the speech of his fellow-countrymen at Lichfield, and that many years of living in the city of London could not alter them. David Garrick, mimicking his old school-master's voice, rolling head and heaving shoulders, once shouted, "Who's for *poonsh?*" to the great joy of the assembled company. One need not labor the point that Johnson was firmly of his time and place, and more than that, was at least two decades behind the moment at which his influence was most deeply felt. If it can be said that one drop of provincialism in a man's blood makes all mankind his kin, then Johnson's heavy frame and swelling veins contained a full pint of that heady liquor. At the moment of his celebrity in London he moved as an ancient Titan in the company of a highly self-conscious and sophisticated group of young and active men; he was the father of their "Literary Club," voicing taboos and parental discriminations among its members; his corpulent figure was the totem of their belief, and his contrasting fits of kindness, or anger, or of despair were the signs of his all-too-human relationship to earth. He entered the latter and declining years of the Augustan Age with the conventions of Queen Anne's day unflawed, untarnished: from the sources of Juvenal, Horace, Dryden, and Pope he drew sustenance for the external forms of his literary style, and it should be added that however well he knew his Greek, his skills were Latin, corresponding to the usefulness, the spans, and masses of the Roman aqueduct. But the melancholy strains within the forms, transfiguring the style and making it his own, were not of the European continent nor of its southern peninsulas:

> Year chases year, decay pursues decay,
> Still drops some joy from with'ring life away.

These strains are of a northern heritage, sounded in the epic of *Beowulf* and heard within the soliloquies of *Hamlet* and *Macbeth*, and their last echoes are resumed beyond Johnson's century in the dramatic verse of Henrik Ibsen. Perhaps it could be said that something which resembles or runs parallel to a *Weltanschauung* has been conveyed within the measures that define the melancholy temper, but we can say that all poetry worthy of our admiration enjoys a happy paradox of seeming most universal when it is most at home, voiced in a language that intones a familiar tongue and is sheltered by the protection of its own roof-tree. In this sense Johnson's major verse as it is represented by *The Vanity of Human Wishes* has elements of greatness that place it within comparable reaches of Gray's *Elegy in a Country Churchyard* and Wordsworth's *Resolution and Independence*. It was Johnson's profound look inward to the passion of life beyond youth and its felicity that endowed his *Human Wishes* with a somber heat, and this perception, however else we may define it, is what we mean when we speak of a writer who possesses "a tragic sense of life."

Of Johnson the moralist—and his morality was of the

8

same root from which his melancholy sprang—it can be said that one finds him less oppressive and certainly less static than he seemed a generation or two ago. His texts for sermons, for the language that he wrote closely resembled the idiom of the pulpit in his day, were drawn from lively observations of the scene around him, a habit which he may have learned from an attentive reading of Dryden and Juvenal, but which, I think, owes a slighter debt to literary influence than to the enforced leisure of his unconquered indolence, to his love of walking through crowded city streets, to his need for company in coffeehouses and to the slow growth of his own literary fame. As indolence increased his sense of guilt, the more urgent was his demand to break its spell, and in that conflict his will was often put to a test of strength between the prospect of lonely hours at his desk or an evening's talk over several bottles of wine. His imitation of Juvenal's *Third Satire*, his *London,* the verses of which Pope had praised and predicted future celebrity for their author, was constantly refreshed and kept in motion by commentary that sharply reflected the diversions of life at the nation's capital. The poem's wealth of contemporary reference was so complete, so vivid in its detail that it has been all too easy for studious readers of it to repeat and to half-accept Sir John Hawkins' claim that "injur'd THALES," who "bids the town farewell," was in fact a portrait of Johnson's old friend, Richard Savage. It seems strange that neither Mr. Smith nor Mr. McAdam sought for a fresh interpretation of the line. For Thales, as we all know, was a wandering Greek philosopher of the seventh century, B.C., who left no writings for posterity. It was he who believed that the single imperishable element of worldly life was water, and the THALES of the poem awaits a boat to take him out to sea; the classical reference ignites the wit that follows after, and we who read the poem today had better forget Sir John's attempt at scholarship and take our stand with Boswell who cheerfully denied THALES's identity with Savage, and who knew his Johnson literally like a book.

In reading Johnson's moral verses we must grant that the very terms of his theology have a further reach toward Heaven and a greater depth than any Thales-like spread through flux and motion; and in reading Johnson generally we should be aware of the penetration, the delicate niceties with which he viewed the weaknesses and merits of his fellow men. The motives behind his observations were avowedly critical, but the results as they appear in his verse and prose place Johnson among the more profound psychologists of his age. The moralist who shouted warnings in Mrs. Thrale's drawing room, and in one instance replied to her nephew's question as to whether or not the young man should marry by saying, "I would advise no man to marry, sir, who is not likely to propagate understanding," was at the very least a lexicographer well-schooled in the flaws of human character. The young man happened to be Sir John Lade, and Johnson afterwards commemorated the occasion of his asking an unfortunate question by writing the famous lines of *A Short Song of Congratulation* which appear in Sir Arthur Quiller-Couch's *Oxford Book of English Verse* under the less ironic title of *One-and-Twenty*. But the fine balance with which Johnson weighed and sustained his judgments of human flaws and virtues was never better exemplified than in the concluding paragraphs of his *Life of Richard Savage*. The sermon was graced by an extraordinarily vital text, and I think I may be pardoned for quoting this particular passage at length, for the delicacy with which Johnson set his scales cannot be shown by citing isolated phrases:

10

He appeared to think himself born to be supported by others, and dispensed from all necessity of providing for himself; he therefore never prosecuted any scheme of advantage, nor endeavored even to secure the profits which his writings might have afforded him. His temper was, in consequence of the dominion of his passions, uncertain and capricious; he was easily engaged and easily disgusted; but he is accused of retaining his hatred more tenaciously than his benevolence.

He was compassionate both by nature and principle, and was always ready to perform offices of humanity; but when he was provoked (and very small offenses were sufficient to provoke him) he would prosecute his revenge with the utmost acrimony till his passion had subsided.

His friendship was therefore of little value; for though he was zealous in the support or vindication of those whom he loved, yet it was always dangerous to trust him, because he considered himself as discharged by the first quarrel from all ties of honor and gratitude, and would betray those secrets which in the warmth of confidence had been imparted to him. This practice drew upon him an universal accusation of ingratitude; nor can it be denied that he was very ready to set himself free from the load of an obligation; for he could not bear to convince himself in a state of dependence, his pride being equally powerful with his other passions, and appearing in the form of insolence at one time and of vanity at another. Vanity, the most innocent species of pride, was most frequently predominant: he could not easily leave off when he had once begun to mention himself or his works; nor ever to read his verses without stealing his eyes from the page, to discover in the faces of the audience how they were affected with any favorite passage.

It is here that we recognize in Richard Savage the character of men who are alive today; the individual and the type have by no means vanished from the earth, and we know them with the same familiarity that we rediscover

Iago, Uncle Toby, Emma Bovary, or Cousin Pons among the faces of our contemporaries. In *Richard Savage* Johnson revealed the springs of human failure, and his creation walks upon a stage where curtains part and footlights gleam beyond the moment of a merely literary being.

Since we are on the subject of Johnson's *Lives of the Poets*, the occasion presents itself for a glance, however brief, at his generally underrated essay on Swift. It is true that Johnson's attitude toward Swift could not be described in terms of unprejudiced affection, for the difference in temperament between the celebrated lexicographer and the late Dean of St. Patrick's would scarcely permit the semblance of a natural rapport. The character of Swift's education whose actual progress took place in Sir William Temple's library was of a seventeenth century order, and in contrast to his tastes and discriminations, the literary preferences of both Pope and Johnson represented the learning of a new generation in English letters. If Johnson leaned backward in time to the conventions of Queen Anne's day, their limitations were fixed by the new order of an Augustan Age which took pride in acknowledging Dryden as its predecessor. The true gulf between Swift and Pope was of a far greater span than Swift's admiration of Pope's genius indicated, so great indeed that an appreciation of the gifts of one is almost certain to obscure the other's. An intelligent comparison of the *Verses on the Death of Dr. Swift* with Pope's *Epistle to Dr. Arbuthnot* is a near impossibility, and the contrast is all the more obvious because the two poems bear a superficial likeness to each other; both delight the reader by a display of self-knowledge beyond all ordinary wit, yet the moment that delight is gratified, the distinctly separate merits of the two poems assert their individuality; as Swift moves backward to Butler's *Hudibras* and ultimately to the rough pleasantries of Skelton, Pope moves forward from Dryden to anticipate the sensibility of William Collins, and from this point onward all comparison becomes irrelevant. Another illustration of the impassable gulf between the imaginations of Pope and Swift is shown in verse written from a common source of literary inspiration. Both poets had read Ovid with unusual insight, but it is significant that Pope chose *The Heroides* on which to model his *Eloisa to Abelard*, while Swift turned to the *Metamorphoses* for the inspiration of his *Baucis and Philemon*. In his *Baucis* Swift ran closer to the effects produced by the graphic art of Hieronymus Bosch, and incidentally to the twentieth century of Max Ernst and Ives Tanguy than to the world of Pope's *Eloisa* and his *Elegy to the Memory of an Unfortunate Lady*. A quotation from the transformation scene in *Baucis* clearly shows the trend of Swift's direction:

> The Groaning Chair began to crawl
> Like an huge Snail along the Wall;
> There stuck aloft, in Publick View,
> And with small Change, a Pulpit grew.
>
> The Porringers, that in a Row
> Hung high and made a glitt'ring Show,
> To a less Noble Substance chang'd,
> Were now but Leathern Buckets rang'd.
>
> The Ballads pasted on the Wall
> Of *Joan* of *France*, and *English Moll*,
> Fair *Rosamond*, and *Robin Hood*,
> The *Little Children in the Wood:*
> Now seemed to look abundance better,
> Improv'd in Picture, Size, and Letter;
> And high in Order plac'd, describe
> The Heraldry of ev'ry Tribe.

A Bedstead of the Antique Mode,
Compact of Timber many a Load,
Such as our Ancestors did use,
Was Metamorphos'd into Pews;
Which still their ancient Nature keep;
By lodging Folks dispos'd to sleep.

The Cottage by such Feats as these,
Grown to a Church by just Degrees,
The Hermits then desir'd their Host
To ask for what he fancy'd most:
Philemon, having paus'd a while,
Return'd them Thanks in Homely Stile;
Then said; my House is grown so Fine,
Methinks, I still wou'd call it mine:
I'm Old, and fain wou'd live at Ease,
Make me the *Parson*, if you please.

I can think of no further reach away from the scene of magic which took place in Philemon's cottage than the following lines from *Eloisa to Abelard*, which are as distant, let us say, as the sight of earth from Eloisa's Heaven:

Grace shines around her with serenest beams,
And whisp'ring angels prompt her golden dreams.
For her th' unfading rose of Eden blooms,
And wings of seraphs shed divine perfumes;
For her the spouse prepares the bridal ring;
For her white virgins hymeneals sing;
To sounds of heavenly harps she dies away,
And melts in visions of eternal day.

It is plain enough (as I have more than hinted in the contrasts of Swift's verse with Pope's) that the *Life of Swift* reflects the same cast of mind which steered Johnson's hand as he wrote his famous remarks on the metaphysical poets of the seventeenth century, but the essay, more than all else, is refined and tempered by the need to present the case of Swift with decent clarity and justice; it would be difficult to unsay Johnson's tributes to Swift's originality, or to quarrel with his apt and highly complimentary report of Swift's character from the confidences of Dr. Delany to Lord Orrery. The point is that even here where Johnson's heart was not warmed by his subject, his scale of values was as delicately set as in his *Life of Richard Savage*, and from that balance we find a definition of Swift's style which has not been improved upon since the day that it was written:

His delight was in simplicity. That he has in his works no metaphor, as has been said, is not true; but his few metaphors seem to be received rather by necessity than choice. . . . His sentences are never too much dilated or contracted; and it will not be easy to find any embarrassment in the complication of his clauses, any inconsequence in his connections, or abruptness in his transitions.

But Johnson's moral instrument, however finely tempered it came to be, was uncommonly slow in taking its proper shape, and surely in the writing of his own verse, Johnson cannot be credited with the brilliance nor accused of the sins of an unlearned precocity. His mistaken venture into poetic drama, his *Irene*, was an early work over which he labored intermittently for ten years. Its production by David Garrick at the Theatre Royal in 1749 crowned its failure, and in the present edition of Johnson's *Poems*, Messrs. Smith and McAdam have erected a veritable Gothic monument of notes over its fallen ruins—a monument, by the way, so attractively placed and garnished that it would have delighted the eye and wit of Horace Walpole. The entire story of the play is told at length, including a memorable quotation from Richard Knolles's *The Generall Historie of the Turkes* from which Johnson received his inspiration, his plot, and the not unseductive figure of his heroine, the beautiful Greek captive, Irene, who had become chief concubine in the household of Sultan Mahomet II. The Sultan's sacrifice of, his murder in fact, of Irene—and this was to appease the critics of his inactivity in war—was neither a happy subject for Johnson's speculations on moral conduct nor was it convincing proof of his heroine's virtues. Nor were Johnson's abilities as a dramatic poet of sufficient energy to convert his lengthy and (it must be admitted) awkward phrasing of moral dialogues into scenes of action. His fortunate choice of epithet in writing verse was of a late maturity and one finds its best examples in the poems written some thirty odd years after the evening which made public *Irene's* disaster in Drury Lane.

We reread Johnson for his last words rather than his first; and among them his *Irene* and *The Vanity of Human Wishes*, which were presented to public view in the same year, may be looked upon today as signs of a turning point in his literary development. The melancholy strains so distinctly overheard throughout the measures of *The Vanity of Human Wishes* continue their progress in the themes of his shorter verses. As Johnson passed the meridian of middle age, his temperament was emphatically less humanitarian than it was humane, and in this distinction we rediscover the high values that he found in masculine courage, individual integrity, and a devotion to the Christian faith. In his later verse it can be said that he practiced what he preached, and indeed the writing of his verses seemed to improve as the slowly growing volume of his prose enlarged from *An Account of the Life of Mr. Richard Savage* in 1744, through *Rasselas* in 1759, to the *Lives*

16

of the Poets in 1779. Even if we remained unaided by Boswell's biography, the course of Johnson's mature development in verse could be traced in parallel lines to the greater exercise of his critical gifts in prose. It would seem that the authority of one proceeds from the other, until at last we are rewarded by *A Short Song of Congratulation* and his verses *On the Death of Dr. Robert Levet.*

Today we reread them in a friendly spirit, for since the passage of the last two decades, even the unwary reader of verse is considerably less frightened by the presence of a critical attitude as it reveals itself in poetry; and I would say that the discovery of moral aphorisms concealed in verse is far less distressing today than it was before the arrival of poetry written by—to name three dissimilar poets —Thomas Hardy, E. A. Robinson, and Mr. T. S. Eliot. Despite Johnson's positive mistrust of metaphysical poets, the revival of their work which caused voluble excitement in literary circles twenty-five years ago, actually paved the road for a renewed awareness of his own merits. The step between a poetry that admits the existence of metaphysical realities and the poetry that expresses the need for religious devotion has always been a short one: in both the presence of a matured poetic intelligence is often happily fused with the creative heat of poetic imagination. It is that intelligence which we rediscover in the following stanzas from Johnson's elegy on Dr. Levet, and in finding it, we are led to appreciate its manly attitudes of religious devotion as well as its sensibility which links the moment of its composition to the poetic imagination of our own day:

> Well tried through many a varying year,
> See Levet to the grave descend;
> Officious, innocent, sincere,
> Of ev'ry friendless name the friend.

. . . . .

When fainting nature call'd for aid,
And hov'ring death prepar'd the blow,
His vig'rous remedy display'd
The power of art without the show.

.   .   .   .   .

His virtues walk'd their narrow round,
Nor made a pause, nor left a void;
And sure th' Eternal Master found
The single talent well employ'd.

After reading these lines it is not too much to say that
the profound depth of Johnson's piety found its most felicitous expression in a last tribute to the friend who once
shared his apartments in Bolt Court—the chaste, industrious,
and almost anonymous London physician whose round of
practice remained among the poor and was circumscribed
by poverty.

Of the many adaptations from Horace that Johnson
wrote, none has greater claim to merit than the one which
is said to have been written within the last month of his
life, on the sixteenth of November, 1784; and since Johnson's imitations of Horace are not generally known, it
seems appropriate to make a full quotation of it here. The
fifteenth and sixteenth lines as well as the last two couplets
are among the best examples of imitation from the Latin
that the eighteenth century has produced, and these were
written in an age that regarded Horace as its master and
imitation of his work as a fine art:

The snow dissolv'd no more is seen,
The fields, and woods, behold, are green,
The changing year renews the plain,
The rivers know their banks again,
The spritely Nymph and naked Grace
The mazy dance together trace.

The changing year's successive plan
Proclaims mortality to Man.
Rough Winter's blasts to Spring give way,
Spring yields to Summer's sovereign ray,
Then Summer sinks in Autumn's reign,
And Winter chills the World again.
Her losses soon the Moon supplies,
But wretched Man, when once he lies
Where Priam and his sons are laid,
Is naught but Ashes and a Shade.
Who knows if Jove who counts our score
Will toss us in a morning more?
What with your friend you nobly share
At least you rescue from your heir.
Not you, Torquatus, boast of Rome,
When Minos once has fix'd your doom,
Or Eloquence, or splendid birth,
Or Virtue shall replace on earth.

Hippolytus unjustly slain
Diana calls to life in vain,
Nor can the might of Theseus rend
The chains of hell that hold his friend.

To read the verse of Johnson's declining years is to hear
the voice of a singularly compact and unified literary personality, and I need not, I hope, insist that even in a literature and language which carry within them many diverse
figures of a vital and enduring individuality, the phenomenon of a Samuel Johnson is extremely rare. Few writers
have achieved his "integration of personality" (the phrase
belongs to Dr. C. G. Jung, but my figure remains the
corpulent lexicographer who received an honorary LL.D.
from Oxford); and that state of being is perhaps the most

frequently cherished hope of the individual of the present age. In England of the eighteenth century Johnson shared with Fielding and Smollett and even Laurence Sterne the will and authority, the patriarchal strength and tenderness of a wholly masculine genius that has not made its reappearance in British literature of the first order since the death of Thomas Hardy. The vigor of an indigenous wit that Boswell heard when Johnson remarked, "The Irish are a FAIR people, they never speak well of one another," has no voice among living Englishmen today; and since the present edition of his *Poems* has received high praise and affectionate regard in the British press, we can be assured that the voice is not forgotten among a people who have outfaced the terrors of a total war.

ON JOHN CLARE, AND THE SIGHT OF
NATURE IN HIS POETRY

IT has taken a hundred years to rediscover John Clare. He himself had lost his name and drifted into madness: was he a poet or merely the son of an impoverished Northamptonshire tenant-farmer, or both or neither? There was a time in London, when no one could afford to say he had not read the *Poems Descriptive of Rural Life and Scenery*, but that was in the spring of 1820, and the season of celebrity was often quite as short then as it is today. Seventeen years later he was to deny his identity, and after that denial, he refused to recognize his wife and children. He was to say that he had been married in spirit to another woman, now long dead: and was he Lord Byron or John Clare?

We must return again to the spring of 1820. There, in the same room that shelters the death mask of John Keats, that moment is restored on canvas in the National Portrait Gallery of London. The portrait is by W. Hilton, R.A. (and he, too, is forgotten) and there we see a young man with sun-bleached golden hair: the pale blue eyes, the thin nostril and slightly parted lips, each feature delicately and sharply turned. He had come up to London in late winter, up to the noisy city of new faces, up from the village of Helpstone in Northamptonshire. A local bookseller, Edward Drury, had advanced him money in payment for the right to publish all his poems and then resold the copyright to prosperous John Taylor, the London publisher.

The advantages of having Taylor for publisher were obvious: Taylor had befriended Keats and had a quick eye for merit in poetry. The disadvantages were far less discernible. Taylor saw in Clare a chance for immediate return upon a small investment and therefore publicized the poet and his book as a literary curiosity. Perhaps Taylor took his cue from the spectacular success of Burns in Edinburgh: here was another peasant with a book of poems, an exotic, handsome figure in a homespun smock under an ill-fitting greatcoat to be made the sensation of a London season. It was evident that Clare was fixed in Taylor's mind as so much commercial property and the first reviews encouraged sales which extended rapidly into a third edition. This premature success was to work against Clare's subsequent reputation, for Clare as the object of literary curiosity was to deflect attention from the true merit of his poetry.

For a few months Clare enjoyed the surprise of being famous:

> To think that I in humble dress
> Might have a right to happiness
> And sing as well as greater men;
> And then I strung the lyre again
> And heartened up o'er toil and fear
> And lived with rapture everywhere,
> Till dayshine to my themes did come.

Yet, for all the promise of success in London, he became uneasy in city lodgings. Charles Lamb was cheerful company and kind; even the remote Lake poets, Coleridge, Southey, Wordsworth, even Byron, sent him their latest books, "bound for the author" and autographed in welcome to the farmer poet. Patrons were eager for nomination in his honor, yet Clare was impatient to be home again, back at Helpstone to the place he knew and cherished. He was to leave London suddenly, breaking an appointment with Taylor to meet Keats: the reason, so he said, was the climax of his determination to marry "Patty" Turner of Walkherd Lodge, nearby his father's farm in Northamptonshire.

At this moment, Clare's future seemed assured: Lord Radstock had invested capital on which the poet was to draw an annual income; another patron, a Mrs. Emmerson, was to watch over him, to send him gifts, to send him friendly letters, to give him, in short, that surplus of benevolence that a kindly English gentry, moved by eccentricity or whim, so often bestows upon the "worthy poor," with the understanding that such beings are admittedly inferior. I doubt if anyone could have foreseen the events which were to follow, could have known that Lord Radstock's investment was to yield but a few pounds a year, the interest steadily declining. Few, if any, could have read those warnings of disaster which attended the early stages of Clare's career: the roots of madness were well concealed, and Clare's bright moment of hopefulness outshone all premonitions of destined failure and obscurity.

It would be mere sentimentality to say that Clare's childhood was unhappy; he was frail but active—yet such happiness must be measured only in terms of the physical beauty of Helpstone. His father's farm, like many another in that neighborhood, had made futile effort toward survival under the shadow of the Enclosure Laws. There, in the calm expanse of the English countryside, relative independence was changed to actual slavery; the farmer was forced to carry an intolerable burden of debt, leaving his heirs a heritage of poverty. The unseen blight was on every blade

23

of grass and in the swelling heart of every grain of corn.

Under this shadow, one incident in Clare's later boyhood was to leave its mark. One day at haying time, the boy saw a farm hand killed by a sharp fall from his wagon. Clare became distraught and fell ill, and for some years following, in spring and autumn, the vivid scene of death in the haying field would float before his eyes: work became impossible, and suddenly sick, faint, defeated, he would leave the plow or scythe until his head cleared and the fit was over. The accurate (and in this instance, painful) memory of realistic detail which was to shape the character of his poetry demanded its toll here; and his emotional sensitivity, so valuable in his development as a poet, was to impede his efficiency in manual labor. Judging from his record of many small jobs held and lost, we may conclude that Clare was an inept farmer; he was too easily distracted by contemplation of a field or flower or by the reading of highly treasured books, among which he listed Thomson's *Seasons*, Goldsmith's *Deserted Village*, Milton's *Paradise Lost* and a translation into English of Aristotle.

Even at this time some hint of what was to become a divided personality might well have dropped into his mind. It was to rise to the surface of his journal on his first trip to London: there, "lolling in a coach," he was to see himself as another person, more talented than honest farmer John, and immeasurable degrees more fortunate. Clearly he saw the relative position of his class in English society, so clearly that Lord Radstock caused ten lines of an attack upon the gentry to be deleted from Clare's early poem, *Helpstone*. But the personal problem (the penumbra in which the farmer left off and the poet began) was a matter of inward confusion and a source of speculation.

It was a problem that gave birth to what might well have seemed a contradiction: though dependent upon patronage and the continued good will of his publisher, the poet, Clare, gained an easy promise of material livelihood; the farmer, Clare, who had retained the sturdiness of the Anglo-Saxon freedmen, also retained the memory of complete independence which was the ambition of his ancestors, and supported "the radical slang" that Lord Radstock discovered in his poetry. Yet it was plain that Clare, the man, was to share (with other tenant-farmers) the unequal burden of economic maladjustment. As peasant he was to observe that inequality, and with other Romantic poets of his time, to assert his independence as an Englishman by writing his convictions into poetry. He was to go mad before a solution of this seeming paradox appeared.

After the London visit of 1820 city patrons would come down to Helpstone to see how a peasant worked and wrote his poetry. Clare was genuinely shy of such patronage and sometimes openly resentful. Like many another self-educated man, he had penetrated to certain unexpected depths of learning and was impatient with a patronage that took for granted a fact that he was no more than a public curiosity. Fearful of those who came to see merely a Helpstone wonder, he would vanish quickly from the small cottage to get outdoors.

On subsequent short, infrequent trips to London (there to visit Lamb, or Hood, or his publisher) he would be silent, sitting in a corner, worrying about money for his wife and children, while in his brain would reappear the scenes of Helpstone: minute photographs of flowers, insects, birds, the clear sky over them and underfoot thick grass and through the fields small rivers flowing.

In ten years his London celebrity was gone and there

25

was great delay in publishing his books. The British public, that had read the new poetry of the time and had welcomed Clare, now swung its mind to other things: to romances by the author of *Waverley*, then to Bulwer-Lytton, to economics, to Carlyle, and last to the novels of Charles Dickens. Meanwhile, Clare had come into his heritage as tenant-farmer, and as his family grew, debts closed around him, and the shadow of poverty over Helpstone loomed deep and wide. At a final moment (then too late) a patron intervened; Clare and his wife and children were removed from the cottage at Helpstone to more comfortable quarters at Northborough. The move, though well-intentioned, contributed further to growing symptoms of insanity; Clare was not "at home"; even this short removal from the place where he knew every foot of ground, seemed to increase his terror, seemed to hasten the birth of another John Clare who transfigured the memory of an adolescent love affair into a present state of being, and who denied the existence of his wife and children.

In 1837 the forgotten poet was committed to a private asylum from which he escaped to Northborough, through Epping Forest on foot for three days and nights of continuous walking, with no stop for food and no time for rest. His condition was hopeless; the image of Mary Joyce, a friend of his early manhood, was stronger than ever, and against the will of his courageous wife, he was finally committed to the charity asylum of Northampton.

The rest of Clare's life is a history of literary discovery. In 1920 Edmund Blunden and Alan Porter edited, chiefly from manuscript, a selection of poems by John Clare. This selection, admittedly inadequate, was an effort to put Clare's best foot forward; more than all else, its purpose was to call attention to the poems, to overbalance the weight of legend and sentimentality set in motion by Frederick Martin's *Life* of 1865. The early Georgian poets, principally Edward Thomas, knew of Clare and set him up as a local deity; he was to aid them in their rediscovery of English countryside as a subject for poetry; his realism, his "botanizing," gained favor with young poets who had rejected the late Victorian interiors of Stephen Philips and the backward-glancing imagination of the Pre-Raphaelites. But the great bulk of Clare's poetry remained in manuscript, in archives at Peterborough and Northborough, and it has taken fifteen years of research started by Mr. Blunden and completed by Mr. J. W. Tibble to arrange and publish some eight hundred poems in legible order.

In learning John Clare's language some patience is required. Judge Clare by a Wordsworthian scale of values, and it would seem that he had no philosophy; compare him with Byron and he would be found lacking in brilliance and personality; contrast him with Keats and he seems provincial and (as Keats himself remarked) "Description too much prevails over the sentiment." In other words, Clare founded his esthetic upon a premise that refuted the work of his contemporaries. He was to write his own answer to Keats by saying:

Keats keeps up a constant allusion (or illusion) to the Grecian mythology, and there I cannot follow . . . where behind every rose bush he looks for a Venus and under every laurel a thrumming Apollo . . . he often described Nature as she appeared to his fancies, and not as he would have described her had he witnessed the things he described.

The positive statement of this same esthetic is made in his *Pastoral Poesy*:

> True poesy is not in words,
>   But images that thoughts express. . . .

27

> A language that is ever green,
>   That feelings unto all impart
> As hawthorne blossoms, soon as seen,
>   Give May to every heart.

Clare's earliest poetry was a direct outgrowth from eighteenth century models: Thomson's *Seasons* and Goldsmith's *Deserted Village* were rewritten in a new setting, and the unwary reader is inclined to agree with Keats, for many of Clare's poems open with a sentiment proper to eighteenth century verse and then wheel precipitously into factual description. After thirty lines are accomplished and almost without warning, the poem becomes Clare's own: "Description" becomes the "sentiment," both are closely interlaced and the visual image is registered upon the reader's brain before there is any consciousness of "meaning."

> Snows on snows in heaps combine,
> Hillocks, rais'd as mountains, shine,
> And at distance rising proud,
> Each appears a fleecy cloud.

So much for the winter scene: then this for a *Summer Evening*.

> Flowers now sleep within their hoods,
> Daisies button into buds;
> From soiling dew the buttercup
> Shuts his golden jewels up;
> And the rose and woodbine they
> Wait again the smiles of day.

In these poems Clare's world of natural objects becomes a world seen under a magnifying glass; at first each object seems minute, then quickly, growing, flowers open and close again and small birds suddenly alive and clear, break into song. Clare's flaw, of course, is rapid composition; in the earlier poems tens of lines are wasted; he was prodigal of both subject matter and vocabulary. However, his use of plain language, the very diction of the countryside in which he lived, preserves for us the vividness of a first impression. Clare's early period closes with a group of lyric narratives which contain *My Mary* (not to be confused with later "Marys") and *Dolly's Mistake*, two poems which not unlike *The Jolly Beggars* of Robert Burns and John Skelton's *The Tunnynge of Elynour Rummynge* owe their vitality, both in language and choice of subject, to strict representation of the lowest levels of society. The drawing is coarse and the humor broad, but the characters live by their own volition, and though they pretend to be no more than creatures of a specific time and locality, they are always contemporaneous; in them a universal law of human mortality is always re-enacted.

Perhaps one word should be said of Clare's satire, *The Parish*. Briefly, Clare had little gift for satire, but he saw, not without terror, not without blunt-edged bitterness, the topheavy structure of a society above him. Among the shorter rural narratives there is a lively recitation of a brawl between recruiting sergeants and the Helpstone peasantry. Again his love of exact detail seems to guide his hand, and the description of an alehouse brawl has something of the same memorable quality (sentimentality and all) which distinguishes Hogarth's *March to Finchley*.

The pre-asylum poetry was to reach its climax in *Summer Images*; here was a poem that surpassed the observation of a Wordsworth and even outglanced the perceptive eye of Wordsworth's sister, Dorothy. It is one of the few poems that Clare is known to have rewritten thoroughly, and between the writing of the first and second versions, his art matured. From this time onward, he knew what his poetic intentions were, and I believe that his subsequent insanity was, in a measure, a means of protecting his right to continue his career as a poet. If we remember that Coleridge relieved the strain of domestic responsibility and checked the pain of neuralgia by generous doses of laudanum, and then assumed what Mr. T. S. Eliot has called the "vocation of a failure," we may grant that Clare, under equal pressure, tended to withdraw from a world that deflected the authority of his poetic vision. Meanwhile he rewrote his *Summer Images*:

> I love at early morn, from new-mown swath,
>   To see the startled frog his route pursue,
> And mark while, leaping o'er the dripping path,
>   His bright sides scatter dew;
> And early lark that from its bustle flies
>   To hail his matin new;
>   And watch him to the skies:
>
> And note on hedgerow haulks, in moisture sprent,
>   The jetty snail creep from the mossy thorn,
> With earnest head and tremulous intent,
>   Frail brother of the morn,
> That from the tiny bents and misted leaves
>   Withdraws his timid horn,
>   And fearful vision weaves.

Clare was to continue writing at this level beyond the publication of his last book, *The Rural Muse*, which was issued and rapidly forgotten in the year 1835.

Clare's loss of identity necessitated a change in his literary personality, and how much of his madness was willed in self-defense may be gathered from these lines:

Free from the world I would a prisoner be
And my own shadow all my company:

And lonely see the shooting stars appear,
Worlds rushing into judgement all the year.

A new John Clare was in the making, another poet who
built the symbol of existence in a madhouse around the
image of his singular madonna, Mary. In the first stages of
his madness, his choice of Mary contained the same de-
fiant guilt-consciousness of Byron's *Manfred*. It was some
time before he was to realize his new personality in terms
of poetry above the level of mere violence, for the Byronic
attitude had led him into a world of false emotions, into
histrionic mannerisms and the darkness of self-pity.

Clare's countryside had changed into "this Hell and
French Bastille of English Liberty," which were the
asylum walls, but there, in that small world, he was to re-
gain his peculiar intensity of vision:

Say, wilt thou go with me, sweet maid,
Say, maiden, wilt thou go with me
Through the valley-depths of shade,
Of night and dark obscurity;
Where the path has lost its way,
Where the sun forgets the day,
Where there's nor light nor life to see,
Sweet maiden, wilt thou go with me?
Where stones will turn to flooding streams,
Where plains will rise like ocean's waves,
Where life will fade like visioned dreams
And mountains darken into caves,
Say, maiden, wilt thou go with me
Through this sad non-identity,

Where parents live and are forgot,
And sisters live and know us not?

Then note:

Say, maiden, can thy life be led
To join the living and the dead?
Then trace thy footsteps on with me;
We are wed to one eternity.

In these last poems which he was to write until his death
in the Northampton asylum in 1864, there is a purity of
diction that recalls the early Blake. His affinity to William
Cowper was expressed in one of the finest elegies of the
day:

Cowper, the poet of the fields
  Who found the muse on common ground—
The homesteads that each cottage shields
  He loved—and made them classic ground.

.   .   .   .   .

Who travels o'er those sweet fields now
  And brings not Cowper to his mind?
Birds sing his name in every bough,
  Nature repeats it in the wind.

And every place the poet trod
  And every place the poet sung
Are like the Holy Land of God,
  In every mouth, on every tongue.

And, like Cowper, he had become the "self-consumer of
his woes"; his haven had become in fact, the madhouse,
which was for him, even to the last, the "Ivory Tower,"
the abiding refuge of the poor.

ON PROSE WRITTEN BY POETS AND, IN
PARTICULAR, ON BYRON'S LETTERS

IT may seem gratuitous to remark that a critical enjoyment of Byron's work necessitates the reading of his letters as well as an appreciation of *Don Juan*, but the fact remains that for the past thirty years, few people have actually read Byron or know him at first hand. I say "few people"—and here I cheerfully exempt all those who read selections from his verse in junior colleges and in universities, and with them I exempt their lecturers and teachers who reread and reinterpret Byron because of his position in Romantic literature. Most of us have been content to read the growing literature surrounding Byron's name: Lord Lovelace's *Astarte*, Ethel Colburne Mayne's definitive biography, or more recently, Peter Quennell's enlivening commentary on the Byronic legend, *Byron: The Years of Fame* and *Byron in Italy* in which the charm that Byron exerted over his contemporaries is revived and presented to us in the light of twentieth century sensibility. If anything, we know the details of Byron's physical appearance, his private maladjustments, and his dramatic entrances into and exits out of public favor a shade too well. True as it may be that Byron lived literature as well as wrote it, it is a salutary exercise to rediscover what he wrote, to reread his prose as well as his best verse, and to recalculate the distance at which he stood from Keats and Shelley, Beddoes and Wordsworth, Coleridge and Southey.

With the notable exceptions of Poe, Emerson, and Coleridge, the poets of the early nineteenth century are scarcely remembered for distinction to be found within their prose. We have nothing here to compare with the richness and dramatic intensity of the prose in Shakespeare's later plays, or with the seasoned wit of Ben Jonson's *Discoveries*. Despite the wealth of commentary on Shakespeare, perhaps too little notice has yet been given to the prose which endowed Iago with a set of nerves and Pandarus with harsh, if not endearing, wit. We also know that little prose writing among poets of Byron's newly arrived nineteenth century could equal the quality and texture of Sir Phillip Sidney's *Arcadia* or of John Donne's sermons. Shelley's prose is thin, boyish, shrill and stiff as though it had inherited the rhetorical flourishes of the century preceding it without bodily force or character; Wordsworth's prose, aside from the famous *Preface* over which he labored and almost fell ill with the effort to sustain his own eloquence, is all too frequently weighted with the sense of its author's importance among the Lake Poets of his generation.

In general, the prose of poets who lived through the period of Britain's Napoleonic Wars suffered the casualties of a transition from an Augustan Age to the Romantic; the balanced periods of Burke, Gibbon, and Samuel Johnson fell out of joint, but the sound of its rocking-horse overtones persisted, and in particular, Shelley's prose carried within it many of the disasters that marked the writing of the time. Perhaps some allowances should be made for Shelley's youth (for there are moments when we are likely to forget how immature the young Wordsworth and Keats and Shelley were) but it is more important to remember the kind of youth that Shelley was. His *Hymn to Intellectual Beauty* was rightly named because its author was a young intellectual of the most enthusiastic sort; he was less

34

learned than swift and eager in his reading, always comprehending the naked scaffolding of an idea rather than its architectural fulfillment. His letters, journals and footnotes sketch the scene, and the reader must apply his own imagination so as to fill the picture; meanwhile, the writer had left earth behind him to ride the light-beams, winds, and clouds of a new theory.

Within the brief era that embraced the active lives of both young poets, no greater contrast can be found than that which distinguishes Shelley's prose from Byron's. Even a temporal distance seems to intervene between them, for among the contrasts, we are overly conscious of the dates which fix the moment of Shelley's letters, while Byron's are as fresh as though they were posted yesterday. Introspective as Byron may have been in *Manfred*, as he wrote his letters * he stood with both feet on an earth that was known by its physical realities, its painted Turkish boys with "large black eyes," its exchanges in money equal to the British guinea, its swimming time—an hour and ten minutes—across the Hellespont, and its eternal presence in the life of literary men. "London," he wrote, "and the world is the only place to take the conceit out of a man—" and then went on to say:

Scott . . . is gone to the Orkneys in a gale of wind;—during which wind, he affirms, the said Scott, "he is sure, is not at his ease,—to say the best of it." Lord, Lord, if these home-keeping minstrels had crossed your Atlantic or my Mediterranean, and tasted a little open boating in a white squall—or a gale in "the Gut"—or the "Bay of Biscay" with no gale at all—how it would enliven and introduce them to a few of the sensations!—to say nothing of an illicit amour or two upon

* *The Letters of Lord Byron*, selected by R. G. Howarth. With an introduction by André Maurois. New York: E. P. Dutton and Company, 1933.

shore, in the way of essay upon the Passions, beginning with simple adultery, and compounding it as they went along.

This is the Byron that Matthew Arnold saw when he spoke of "that true and puissant personality, with its direct strokes, its ever-welling force, its satire, its energy." It was also the Byron whom Goethe recognized, was refreshed by the encounter, and of whom was impelled to say, no other poet *"der ihm zu vergleichen wäre."* The singularity which Goethe was so happy to acknowledge lies at the heart of some two hundred and eighty letters selected from complete editions of Byron's prose.

Byron's energy, even in its surplus, was unique; it forced his growth from a bright and restless school boy at Harrow and Trinity College at Cambridge, into a citizen of the world who knew the Near East with the same glancing familiarity which accompanied his arrival in a drawing room at Holland House; its electric stream overflowed the pages of *Childe Harold*, the *Hebrew Melodies*, the *Oriental Tales* into a daylight world of action, into his letters, into grandiose schemes of travel, and last to a road which led to the battlefield at Missolonghi. Many of the letters were written, like the rapid cantos of *Don Juan*, because he could not stop the flow. At home he wrote and spoke openly of the boredom, the confusion, the excitements into which his domestic life had fallen; abroad, a like impulse caused him to record his entrances into each foreign setting, noting events and details of scenery, of habits and dress of men and women as he rode by. With rather more than a shrewd guess at the proportions of the world within his glance, he measured all against himself. This world, of course, was the very map of Europe which had been so recently traversed by dreams of Napoleonic conquest, and was now entered, scrawled with the percentage marks of loss and profit on its margins, within the balance sheets of the House of Rothschild.

It is often difficult to think of anything that Byron wrote as being schooled in any art, of being subject to training, or to use a more forbidding term, restraint. Beyond their hastily acknowledged obligations to stanza forms, the cantos of *Childe Harold* and *Don Juan* literally wander behind the footsteps of their heroes; even the felicities—and nearly matchless ease—of his brief lyric, *So, We'll Go No More A Roving*, have the charm of spontaneity and the air of seeming archly accidental. Yet training, as we all know, Byron possessed, and Paul Elmer More was by no means wrong in attributing Byron's qualities of clarity and force to his admiration for the satires of Alexander Pope. Byron's early satires, written in boyish imitation of Pope's hand, are scarcely worth the effort of rereading; it is not until we reach the cantos of *Don Juan* that we see how brilliantly, how knowingly the skill, the conversational tact of Pope's *Epistle to Dr. Arbuthnot* had been assimilated. Byron wore his early schooling in Pope's satires as briskly as a cloak thrown back across his shoulders; and even to this day the gesture half-annoys, half-charms the reader. Its meretricious qualities were obvious, but the gaudy phrase and image, the insensitive diction caught the eye and ear of his feminine admirers and imitators, who from L. E. L. to our contemporary, Miss Millay, traced the vicissitudes of the Byronic gesture in their own verse. What was less obvious, and what his imitators lacked, was the strength and clarity of his critical genius. It was Byron's critical aptitude flowing at the same speed with which his hand guided a pen across a sheet of paper that enlivens many a canto of *Don Juan* and gives life to even the most casual of his hastily written letters.

As if to balance the recurrent fits of self-castigation, of

torpor, and then renewed restlessness in Italy, stood the security of his own bank account and the fact that he had inherited a title. These last were of the material world that he knew so well and judged so brilliantly; these he remembered to feed his pride, nor did he forget them in viewing his less tangible reputation as a poet. It was in the person of Lord Byron that he wrote to Tom Moore, his friend, and to John Murray, his publisher; and in writing to them it was always clear enough that his fame was something which could be taken for granted, if not ignored. To Moore he stressed his conviction that he was far removed from literary rivalry: "Surely the field of fame is wide enough for all; and if it were not, I would not willingly rob my neighbor of a roof of it." His dislike of Southey was based upon a natural rejection of the gooseberry-tart-home-and-fireside character of Southey's verse, but as for the man himself, Byron was not ungenerous, and in his remarks to Moore one understands why Southey impressed his contemporaries and why his thoroughly mediocre gifts were rewarded by the Laureateship:

Yesterday, at Holland House, I was introduced to Southey—the best-looking bard I have seen in some time. To have that poet's head and shoulders, I would almost have written his Sapphics. He is certainly a prepossessing person to look on, and a man of talent, and all that, and—*there* is his eulogy.

His distrust of Wordsworth also sprang from a difference in intellectual temper; as for the rest, he was willing to praise, and the measure of that praise may be noted in his early recognition of Coleridge, Shelley, and Keats. He urged Murray to publish an anonymous "Anti-Byron": ". . . there is no earthly reason why you should *not*, on the contrary, I should receive it as the fairest compliment *you* could pay my candor." Many of Byron's best letters were addressed to Murray, for the publisher represented the world outside the dark, confused, semi-Faustian facets of Byron's character; to Byron, Murray's world was one of daylight and sanity and the relationship between the two men was kept alive through mutual—and material—profit.

We are not aware of how bad a correspondent Byron could be until we come upon the small cycle of letters to Anne Isabella Milbank. The courtship letters are stiff and dull; and the familiar stream of gossip, incident, and literary opinion seems to have been abruptly checked. One wonders if his rôle of the reformed rake had not been played a shade too well: objectively, Miss Milbank would have made the perfect Lady Byron; she possessed a fortune greater than his, she was by no means unintelligent, and had sufficient social poise to carry his title with ease and youthful dignity. For once, I think, his strong sense of external reality was to defeat its purpose. Because he had made up his mind to neglect the intangibilities of human emotion, both in himself and in his young wife, he was driven back into the mirrored, nightmare world of *Manfred*, and there was faced by his violent and helpless ego. He had seen that very danger in rejecting the advances of Lady Caroline Lamb, but she, of course, had been his female counterpart, a seductive, childish, almost ridiculous copy of himself. The famous Easter Sunday letter addressed to Lady Byron which was written immediately following his break with her shows how far he had miscalculated in reading her character; despair and broken pride punctuated the rapid sentences and phrases, and these were the warnings of a psychic instability that all women fear. The image of *Manfred* rose out of darkness to haunt young Lady Byron, and with him, his mistress and half-sister, the pliable Augusta, but it was a *Manfred* stripped of all power

39

except that which carries wives and daughters down with him.

It is only in the letters to his wife that one reads how closely Byron steered toward the personal disintegration that marked the careers of Baudelaire and Edgar Poe; but it would be dangerous, I think, to speculate too freely on the incident which inspired them, or to overdramatize the process by which he righted himself; yet right himself he did as he left England to resume his travels on the Continent. The last grand tour of eight years had begun: by September 17th, 1816, he was already writing to Augusta, "What a fool was I to marry—and *you* not very wise. . . . Had you been a Nun—and I a Monk—that we might have talked through a grate instead of across the sea—no matter—my voice and heart are ever thine—" He was of one piece again, and wrote to Murray of the guillotine in Rome and how he used an opera glass to see three thieves beheaded.

It was not until 1823 that signs of weariness and nervous irritation began to cloud his outward glancing eye: "I have not been so robustious as formerly," he wrote, "ever since the last summer, when I fell ill after a long swim in the Mediterranean," but to this he added a note of relief from his worry and fear of growing fat, "I am thin—perhaps thinner than when you saw me when I was nearly transparent, in 1812." He was about to shake himself free of the soft arms of the Guiccioli; with Shelley's death one chapter of his Italian holiday had closed; the Leigh Hunts and their children ("They are dirtier and more mischievous than Yahoos," he wrote to Mary Shelley.) had been packed up and sent back home to England. The prospect of an adventurous campaign in Greece became more attractive hourly and a newly shifting map of Europe was underfoot. He perceived that the end of kings and empires was near, and in looking toward that end his vision cleared again:

40

"Give me a republic . . ." he wrote, "there will be blood shed like water and tears like mist, but the peoples will conquer."

There was less of wishful thinking in Byron's prophecy than one might suppose, and I believe that his view was that of the seasoned traveler who for some years had been quick to read the political equation concealed behind the passage of events; eighty years after Byron's death, Wilfred Scawen Blunt possessed the same qualities of specific and realistic insight, and if he lacked the dramatic gifts of personality as well as the poetic talents that Byron so successfully employed, he was no less proficient in discerning the meaning of action behind the smoke-screens of European diplomacy. Byron had little enough respect for the intelligence of a social order that had produced him; and though he showed no contempt for the British guineas that had made him wealthy, he had no intention of leaning backward among the ruins of an old order. Even the phrasing of his prophecy intones the eloquence that is sometimes heard in the phrasing of a military dispatch, as though he had been composing a message to be carried by a telegraph system that was as yet unknown. His executive ability which had hitherto been directed toward the management of a caravan winding its way across Italy, now leaped to generalship; the gesture was toward pure action, action that hoped to leave the ghost of *Manfred* asleep in London, and was to outdistance, if possible, the incompleted career of *Don Juan*. Perhaps this effort sought out the creation of a "pure" Byron, as though it were the last and logical refinement of his energy. Actually, he neared exhaustion and was ill, but the prospect of crowded duties beyond his physical strength effected temporary relief. The tempo of his last letters is of the pace that he had set himself to follow; to those who read them, they seemed mobile and alert, as though the writer had reawakened from a long sleep. In a last note to Murray dated February 25th, 1824, he described the illness that had overtaken him at Missolonghi; the report is characteristically objective, and its accents were as masculine and forthright as Henry Fielding's documentary account of his *Voyage to Lisbon*, a journal, by the way, which was written to divert its author's mind from a fatal and rapidly consuming illness:

. . . but whether it was epilepsy, catalepsy, cachexy, or apoplexy, or what other *exy* or *epsy*, the doctors have not decided . . . but it was very unpleasant and nearly carried me off and all that.

The last echoes of Byron's voice are in the voice of *Don Juan*, the voice of a critical attitude that was spoken in burlesque of the so-called "Byronic spirit" which had greeted the world with the opening cantos of *Childe Harold* in 1812. It has been said often enough that the existence of Byron's mock-hero killed, or at least brought to a period stop, the epic poem in modern literature, and it has also been remarked with increasing frequency that Henri Beyle's *Julien Sorel*, whose end foretold the death of glory in twentieth century heroic attitudes, bore the marks of a strong lineal heritage from *Don Juan*. But beyond these Byron's *Juan* has as many living heirs as Cervantes Saavedra's *Quixote*, and as they multiply the relationship becomes more subtle and infinitely complex. One rediscovers in the disillusionment of Gregers Werle of *The Wild Duck* the answer in prose to Ibsen's *Brand*, as well as to the romantic excesses of *Peer Gynt*, and the *Juan* of Bernard Shaw's *Man and Superman* has a candid alignment with his famous progenitor. So much then may be said for the direct line, but indirectly *Juan's* critical spirit has survived in extraordinary disguise, entering E. A. Robinson's *Miniver*

Cheevy's discontent and disappearing by way of alcohol, only to re-emerge and not without reference to Prince Hamlet in the voice of Mr. T. S. Eliot's *Prufrock*:

I grow old. . . . I grow old. . . .
I shall wear the bottoms of my trousers rolled.

Shall I part my hair behind? Do I dare to eat a peach?
I shall wear white flannel trousers, and walk upon the
    beach.
I have heard the mermaids singing, each to each.

I do not think that they will sing to me.

The deliberate flatness of the last line of my quotation from the lips of Prufrock has a veiled parallel to the breakneck rhymes—the quickening, almost breathless descent into prose—of *Don Juan;* both techniques engender the progress of ironic wit and both depend upon the presence of the critical spirit that creates an emotional tension between the so-called "poetic" imagination and the "antipoetic." The same play of wit is shown in the sharp contrasts of prose and poetry in Shakespeare and one can see and hear its art at work in the great scenes of *Hamlet.* If *Don Juan* is the last and far-reaching illumination of Byron's genius, what of *Manfred*, which despite its attractions as one of the most enduring expressions of the "Romantic Agony," is seldom reread today?

It must be confessed that *Manfred*, measured by the depths of its penetration into the human soul, is a failure. Its flaws embody the flaws of Byron's art and character; the great release of energy that made its conception possible grew impatient, characteristically enough, of a choice of language and intensity of speech that the play demanded. Compared with Milton's *Samson Agonistes* or Baudelaire's *Fleurs du Mal*, or even Rainer Maria Rilke's

Duino Elegies, Manfred's reaches into the heart of human guilt seem superficial. But in the light of *Don Juan* and in reconsideration of Byron's Oriental romances, *Manfred* assumes a far more fortunate aspect; it is then and only then that *Manfred* takes a position of contrapuntal importance of which *Juan's* career and Byron's letters were the true catharsis and critical resolution.

ON THE GOTHIC IMAGINATION IN ROMANTIC
POETRY AND THE SURVIVAL OF THOMAS
LOVELL BEDDOES

IT would be easy, and I believe, several degrees too easy, to speak of Thomas Lovell Beddoes as a lesser Byron. At first glance, Byron and Beddoes seem fortunately linked: both were extraordinarily precocious, both enjoyed the freedom of living away from home in exile on the European continent, both found a release for creative energy in revolutionary politics, both experimented in the writing of poetic drama, and both men welcomed death on foreign shores. But beyond this rough analogy the comparison begins to fail, and indeed it illustrates the not unfamiliar difficulty that has come into being by freely tossing the names of a half-dozen early nineteenth century British poets into undue proximity; in this confusion we find the poetry of Keats and Shelley bound between covers of a single volume in *The Modern Library*, and the same darkness hovers over thoroughly respectable academic discussions of all figures grouped under the heading of "The Romantic Movement." It is all too seldom that true and pertinent distinctions are made within this convenient group of attractive names, for names in close company, like coins jingled too frequently together, lose their faces, and in literary discourse, many names are worn to faceless brilliance in the jargon of studious research and reappreciation.

If the temptation exists to place Beddoes in biographical proximity to Byron, an even greater temptation to view him as a belated Elizabethan has not been resisted. If we could be content with a second glance at Beddoes' works in the huge, eight-hundred-page volume, so devotedly, almost devoutly edited by Dr. H. W. Donner,* we would agree with the reiterated opinions of Lytton Strachey, which were dutifully followed by Mr. F. L. Lucas, and George Saintsbury. All opinions chimed to the belated Elizabethan character of Beddoes' poetry—nor was the epithet entirely without foundation. Beddoes' literary indebtedness to Marlowe, Marston, Webster, and Tourneur was of no inconsiderable weight; he read them with the fascination and joy that Keats described at his discovering Chapman's Homer. In reading for ourselves the shadowed pages and the luminous passages of Beddoes' Gothic mystery play, *Death's Jest-Book*, we are in little danger of forgetting the impress that Marlowe and Webster had left upon them—that is all too obvious, and to deny it would be as futile as denying Wordsworth's debt to Milton. Granting all this, the best of Beddoes' poetry merits a third reading, and in a final consideration a balance may be struck between a Victorian neglect of Beddoes' virtues and the excitement of their rediscovery in the twentieth century.

The story of Beddoes' extraordinary, brief, ineffectual, and obscure career has been told at length in Dr. Donner's definitive biography. Like many a patient, pure-minded labor of love, Dr. Donner's book † has earned respect, if not reciprocal enthusiasm, and its sheets have not been im-

* *The Works of Thomas Lovell Beddoes*, edited with an introduction by H. W. Donner. Oxford University Press, 1935.
† *Thomas Lovell Beddoes: The Making of a Poet*, by H. W. Donner. Basil Blackwell: Oxford, 1935.

ported to this side of the Atlantic. Beddoes' personality was of the same psychic disorder and maladjustment that shaped the behavior of Rimbaud in the nineteenth century and Hart Crane in the twentieth, yet the environment of his early youth was far more fortunate than theirs; he was the son of the prosperous and notoriously eccentric Dr. Thomas Beddoes and a nephew of the witty and gifted Maria Edgeworth. At the age of nineteen and while still an undergraduate at Pembroke College, Oxford, he achieved celebrity through the publication of his play in verse, *The Brides' Tragedy*—and in the second year after Keats' death in 1823, Beddoes received more spontaneous and authoritative praise than any young poet of his generation. Two years later, he had left Pembroke for the University of Göttingen, leaving England, and his "ambition to become poetically distinguished" behind him. Yet, as his friend, Thomas Forbes Kelsall, knew, Beddoes had already started work on the dramatic poem, *Death's Jest-Book*, which was to become the true object of his ambitions and to haunt his imagination for the next twenty years. Kelsall, and another friend, James Dykes Campbell, saw how persistently the growth of *Death's Jest-Book* broke through and was nourished by Beddoes' studies in medicine, and they were also in a position to know, through correspondence, the restless, guilt-haunted temper of Beddoes' intelligence, its release of energy in political oratory at Würzburg, its violence, its ardors, and the reaches of its last expression at its death-bed, "I am food for *what I am good for*—worms."

But even death itself and probable suicide in 1849 (which Dr. Donner establishes as a near-certainty) did not check the pursuit of Nemesis which shadowed Beddoes' fame. Beddoes' misplaced confidence in Bryan Waller

Procter's, "Barry Cornwall's," critical advice, which had smoothly glanced across the surfaces of fragmentary pieces from Beddoes' pen with an impartial lack of understanding, repeated its cycle in 1883 when Robert Browning, who had promised Kelsall that he would edit and publish Beddoes' manuscripts, called in the assistance of Sir Edmund Gosse. Both Sir Edmund and Browning were shocked at what they found within the box that Kelsall left them, and for the moment the incident served only to permit Dykes Campbell to make a transcript of everything the box contained. We shall never be quite clear as to exactly what horrified the sensibilities of Gosse, but we do know that the box and its contents were handed over to the care of Browning's son, and were, thereafter, irrevocably lost. Gosse, with his adroit and habitual negligence, issued an edition of Beddoes' poetry in 1890, and in 1928 another edition appeared, prepared by Gosse and published in a manner that is usually reserved—including an evasive introduction and a garish typeface—for pornographia. Aside from a few scraps of actual manuscript, and a pamphlet of verse in German, what we read today in Dr. Donner's excellent edition of *The Works of Thomas Lovell Beddoes* are the copies made of Beddoes' poems in Dykes Campbell's hand.

Because of the ill-luck which attended the posthumous publication of Beddoes' poetry, it would seem that we approach it with the utmost difficulty—and so we do. Sir Arthur Quiller-Couch's reprinting of a mutilated version of Beddoes' *Dream-Pedlary* in *The Oxford Book of English Verse* increased rather than diminished the general air of confusion which has so persuasively followed mention of Beddoes' name, and the question arises as to where and how the confusion originated. Were Procter, Browning,

48

Gosse, and Sir Arthur wholly responsible for the obscurity of Beddoes' fame? It must be confessed that they materially aided its long career of darkness, but its true source lies in the uneasy relationship which existed between Beddoes and his work; self-knowledge was of slow and fatal growth within him, and when it came, it came too late. There was more of self-realization than of true humility or of pathos in Beddoes' last note to Revell Phillips: "I ought to have been among other things a good poet." It is not enough to say with Dr. Donner that Beddoes lacked self-confidence; the psychic split which marred his character and brought his private life within the area that we reserve for Rimbaud and Hart Crane, ran deeper than any loss of confidence in what he wrote. The attitude that he adopted toward his poetry swung between and often touched the two extremes of desiring an absolute perfection in its expression and the impulse to destroy it utterly, yet the ambition to write voluminously, to be heard, to speak aloud remained. His miscalculation in measuring the quality of Procter's literary friendship could almost be described as an act of literary suicide; it was his sin against the mark of his own genius, which had left its impress upon every brilliant passage that comes to light in the tortured progress of writing *Death's Jest-Book*.

Beyond the sources of literary stimulation which Beddoes received from a reading of the lesser Elizabethan dramatists, was his greater effort to clothe and vitalize the spirit and temper of the Gothic myth, the genius that had created the gargoyles on the towers of Notre Dame, the giantchild Gargantua, the merry voyages of Pantagruel, the fiery journey of Mad Meg across Flanders, the Dance of Death itself (which actually enters a scene of *Death's Jest-Book*), the very genius that had found its revival in

Matthias Claudius' brief and exquisite lyric, *Der Tod und das Mädchen.* Beddoes' prose version of death and the maiden appears in semi-classical disguise in *The Tale of the Lover to his Mistress:*

After the fall of Jupiter came Love one night to Psyche: it was dark in her cottage and she began to strike a light. "Have done," said he, in a low whispering tone—in which the hinge of some dreadful dark truth out of another world seemed to turn. "Youth, power, and heaven have passed away from the gods: the curse of age has changed their shapes:— then seek not to look on me, Psyche; but if thou art faithful, kiss me, and we will then go into the darkness for ever."— "How art thou changed?" asked she; "methinks you do but try me, jestingly, for thou canst only have grown more beautiful. That thou art more powerful I hear, for the night air is full of rushing arrows, and many are struck and sigh. Hast thou lost thy wings that were so glorious?"—"Aye, but I am swifter than of old."—"Thy youth?"—"Aye, but I am stronger: all must fall before me."—"Thy charms and wiles?"—"Aye, but he whom I have once stricken, is mine for ever and ever."— "Why should I not see thee then? Art thou Love no more?"— "Aye, but not fleeting, earthly; eternal, heavenly Love."— Just then the moon rose, and Psyche saw beside her a gaunt anatomy, through which the blue o' th' sky shone and the stars twinkled, gold promises beaming through Death, armed with arrows, bearing an hour-glass. He stepped with her to the sea-side, and they sank where Venus rose.

The attraction that the Gothic imagination held for Beddoes may be sought for well outside the boundaries of his great admiration for Webster, Marston, and Marlowe, and the forces that drew him toward it were as strong as the impulse which Coleridge felt in the writing of *The Rime of the Ancient Mariner:*

Are those her ribs through which the Sun
Did peer as through a grate?
And is that Woman all her crew?
Is that a Death? and are there two?
Is Death that woman's mate?

Her lips were red, her looks were free,
Her locks were yellow as gold:
Her skin was as white as leprosy,
The Nightmare Life-in-Death was she,
Who thicks man's blood with cold.

The genius toward which Beddoes moved was of an elder heritage and of the same, yet deeper root than any reading of the Elizabethan dramatists would disclose; the power of attraction had its true origins behind the façades of Renaissance literature at their noon-tide; Beddoes' effort to recreate a truly Gothic metaphysic from the slowly increasing manuscript of *Death's Jest-Book* was, if anything, kept alive and nurtured by his residence on central European soil, and the impulse which lay behind the creation of his incompleted masterpiece was as clear a symptom of his day as Coleridge's *Ancient Mariner* or Sir Walter Scott's translation of Goethe's remarkable *Erlkönig*. Truly enough *Death's Jest-Book* restrung and hinged together the common properties of Renaissance poetic drama, and among them the network of double plots and motives inspired by revenge, but what is important for us to rediscover is Beddoes' persistent stress upon those elements in Webster and in Marlowe in which the sources ran backward to the Middle Ages; and there it was that Beddoes had made his choice. Like Edgar Poe, Beddoes was a late arrival on the Romantic scene, and like the American poet, his lyricism expressed a last if fragmentary refinement of a first phase in Romantic emotion that had traced its conscious origins to the *Lyrical Ballads* of 1798. His fantastically late resurrection has blurred, almost beyond recognition, his true position within the literature of his day. No echoes of his voice were heard within it beyond the strains of that eminently precocious venture, *The Brides' Tragedy;* and Procter's friendly indifference had closed the door to those in England who might have heard him with a reawakened ear.

Since I have viewed at length the unfortunate aspects of Beddoes' career and its subsequent miscarriages of fame, one should modify that unequitable balance by saying that Dr. Donner's edition of his *Works* appeared at a particularly happy moment for their twentieth century revival. If Beddoes' relationship to his creative gifts and their fulfillment was, to put it mildly, sporadic and uncertain, their radical nature was remarkably consistent. In that respect alone, his life, his work, his political convictions, and the quality of his imagination resemble what we have read in the poems, the letters and notebooks of Gerard Manley Hopkins. Because of the singular likeness in radical temper, it can be said with certain obvious reservations that the discovery of Hopkins' poems immediately following the first World War prepared the critics for a favorable reception of Dr. Donner's edition of Beddoes' *Works.* In the middle 1930's and on both sides of the Atlantic, writers of conservative beliefs as well as left, sought out their origins of a radical heritage, and in this sense the revival of Beddoes' name carried with it associations of particular significance; and Beddoes' participation in revolutionary activity was of a nature that paralleled the activity of young British writers in the recent Spanish Civil War.

Beddoes' career in Germany and Switzerland had been punctuated by the writing of political satires, and the most successful of these were written in his adopted German, a language which he spoke with rapidly increasing facility. They were done as though he were on holiday from his major work in *Death's Jest-Book*, as though the shift in language were a release from the demands of seeking the perfected line, the absolute phrase, the final word. Quite as *The Brides' Tragedy* had achieved distinction as a *tour de force* in the revival of Elizabethan dramatic verse, Beddoes' brilliantly turned political satires served a lively purpose in expressing the radical spirit of his time; among these, there are speeches and verses which were in effect a triple-edged attack on the forces that sanctioned the Holy Alliance, the Church itself, and reactionary German poetry. Quickened by Beddoes' wit and energy the German language was transformed into parody of itself, and what Beddoes had learned from reading Rabelais came to light in his pamphlet which contained verses *On the Enemies of David Friedrich Strauss*, his *Antistraussianischer Gruss*. To find their equal one must turn to John Skelton's satire *Why Come Ye Not to Court* or to certain passages of James Joyce's *Finnegans Wake;* and it is also of historical interest to remember that David Strauss and the incident which inspired the verses left an impression on the early education of Karl Marx. The pamphlet found an appreciative audience among Swiss and German revolutionaries, and its distribution warned educational authorities in central Europe of a certain medical student, Herr Beddoes, a little Englishman, who on one occasion at least had roused fellow students to revolt by reciting a mock tribute to the dying Wellington, "Prussia's one Field Marshal."

How deeply these activities affected the revised versions of *Death's Jest-Book*, we shall never know, but in the play of plot and counter-plot of Beddoes' Gothic melodrama, the forces of established power, of revolution and of counter-revolution run their bloody courses, motivated by revenge. The two Fools in the play (and originally it was sub-titled, *The Fool's Tragedy*) seem to speak in Beddoes' voice and certainly they recite a number of his finest lyrics, but what of Mario, a character who seeks a leader and who speaks with memorable eloquence?

> A Roman am I;
> A Roman in unroman times: I've slept
> At midnight in our Capitolian ruins,
> And breathed the ghost of our great ancient world,
> Which there doth walk: and among glorious visions,
> That the unquiet tomb sent forth to me,
> Learned I the love of Freedom. Scipio saw I
> Washing the stains of Carthage from his sword,
> And his freed poet, playing on his lyre
> A melody men's souls replied unto:
> Oak-bound and laurelled heads, each man a country;
> And in the midst, like a sun o'er the sea
> (Each helm in the crowd gilt by a ray from him),
> Bald Julius sitting lonely in his car,
> Within the circle of whose laurel wreath
> All spirits of the earth and sea were spell-bound.
> Down with him to the grave! Down with the god!
> Stab, Cassius; Brutus, through him; through him, all!
> Dead.—As he fell there was a tearing sigh:
> Earth stood on him; her roots were in his heart;
> They fell together. Caesar and his world
> Lie in the Capitol; and Jove lies there,
> With all the gods of Rome and of Olympus; . . .

Despite the weight of inversions in Mario's speech, despite the rhetorical extravagance of "Down with him to the grave! Down with the god!" which show the marks of

Schiller's influence as well as the intonations of a distinctly unmodulated school of German acting, the speech reveals a clear and vivid strength of movement that distinguishes the best of Beddoes' poetry from the work of his better known contemporaries. The historical imagination which finds its voice within the speech displays an insight of remarkable force and energy, and is of that quality which we associate with the utterance of prophetic truth.

Perhaps *Death's Jest-Book* by the very weight of its intentions was foredoomed to remain imperfect and unfinished; perhaps there is prophetic significance in the shift of its sub-title from *The Fool's Tragedy* to *The Day Will Come*, that is, the day of its completion placed forever in the future. Quite as D. H. Lawrence was never to complete the larger plan of *The Rainbow*, or as Keats's *Hyperion* remains a fragment, or as Hart Crane's *The Bridge* could not attain the elaborated structure of its early inspiration, so *Death's Jest-Book* falls short of its original design. The desire to create a work of all-embracing stature and dimensions is one of the deepest and most frequently noted pitfalls of the Romantic imagination; surely its shadows haunted Coleridge's *Kubla Khan* and his ode *Dejection*, and from then onward the path went downward into the darkness of being unable to write poetry at all. The last days of Beddoes' life were spent in that same darkness, yet before his work can be dismissed as one who "had made failure his vocation," some attention must be given to two short poems, which are, to my knowledge, among the best examples of lyric verse written in Beddoes' generation.

Since the complete version of *Dream-Pedlary* still lacks the public it deserves, and since the quality of its imagination merits its rediscovery in all discussions of nineteenth century poetry, I need not apologize for including an entire quotation of it here:

I

If there were dreams to sell,
  What would you buy?
Some cost a passing bell;
  Some a light sigh,
That shakes from Life's fresh crown
Only a roseleaf down.
If there were dreams to sell,
Merry and sad to tell,
And the crier rung the bell,
  What would you buy?

II

A cottage lone and still,
  With bowers nigh,
Shadowy, my woes to still,
  Until I die.
Such pearl from Life's fresh crown
Fain would I shake me down.
Were dreams to have at will,
This would best heal my ill,
  This would I buy.

III

But there were dreams to sell,
  Ill didst thou buy;
Life is a dream, they tell,
  Waking, to die.
Dreaming a dream to prize,
Is wishing ghosts to rise;
  And, if I had the spell
  To call the buried, well,
    Which one would I?

IV

If there are ghosts to raise,
　　What shall I call,
Out of hell's murky haze,
　　Heaven's blue hall?
Raise my loved longlost boy
To lead me to his joy.
　　There are no ghosts to raise;
　　Out of death lead no ways;
　　　　Vain is the call.

v

Know'st thou not ghosts to sue?
　　No love thou hast.
Else lie, as I will do,
　　And breathe thy last.
So out of Life's fresh crown
Fall like a rose-leaf down.
　　Thus are the ghosts to woo;
　　Thus are all dreams made true,
　　　　Ever to last!

Not even the sensitively gifted Tennyson of *The Lady of Shalott* or of the lyrical interludes in *Maud* quite equals the play of sound and echo, of sight and recall of image that weave and finally complete the garland so gracefully thrown across death's shoulders in *Dream-Pedlary*. One would probably have a better chance of finding an equal among Hölderlin's lyrical remains, rather than in any selection of English poetry, but even there, only the like quality of spirit may be sought and not the melodic variations of Beddoes' lines. In contemporary literature, the nearest approach to Beddoes' lyric imagery may be found in the fol-

lowing lines from Walter de la Mare; the spirit has thinned
and grown remote, but its shadow lingers:

> Not toward Death, who, stranger, fairer,
> Than any siren turns his head—
> Than sea-couched siren, arched with rainbows,
> Where knell the waves of her ocean bed.
> Alas, that beauty hangs her flowers
> For lure of his demoniac powers:
> Alas, that from these eyes should dart
> Such piercing summons to thy heart;
> That mine in frenzy of longing beats,
> Still lusting for these gross deceits.
>   Not that way!

As one reads through the prose and verse fragments of
The Ivory Gate, supposedly written by Beddoes between
the years 1833 to 1838, the likeness of his verse and its
imagery turns in the direction of his distant, and almost certainly unknown to him, American contemporary, Edgar
Poe; unfinished manuscripts bearing the title, *The City of
the Sea* appear, and the best (and apparently completed)
union of prose and verse among the scattered papers is
Thanatos to Kenelm:

"I have no feeling for the monuments of human labour,"
she would say, "the wood and the desart are more peopled
with my household gods than the city or the cultivated country. Even with the living animals and the prevailing vegetation
of the forest in this hemisphere, I have little sympathy. I know
not the meaning of a daisy, nor what nature has symbolized
by the light bird and the butterfly. But the sight of a palm
with its lofty stem and tuft of long grassy leaves, high in the
blue air, or even such a branch as this (breaking off a large
fern leaf) awake in me a feeling, a sort of nostalgy and long-
ing for ages long past. When my ancient sire used to sit with

me under the old dragon tree or Dracaena, I was as happy as the ephemeral fly balanced on his wing in the sun, whose setting will be his death-warrant. But why do I speak to you so? You cannot understand me."—And then she would sing whisperingly to herself:

> The mighty thoughts of an old world
> Fan, like a dragon's wing unfurled,
>   The surface of my yearnings deep;
> And solemn shadows then awake,
> Like the fish-lizard in the lake,
>   Troubling a planet's morning sleep.
>
> My waking is a Titan's dream,
> Where a strange sun, long set, doth beam
>   Through Montezuma's cypress bough:
> Through the fern wilderness forlorn
> Glisten the giant harts' great horn
>   And serpents vast with helmed brow.
>
> The measureless from caverns rise
> With steps of earthquake, thunderous cries,
>   And graze upon the lofty wood;
> The palmy grove, through which doth gleam
> Such antediluvian ocean's stream,
>   Haunts shadowy my domestic mood.

It is highly probable that the speech and its song were originally spoken by Sibylla, one of the heroines of *Death's Jest-Book*, that the song appeared in an early draft of the play's first act, and was later discarded from the revised versions. Like many passages within the play, the speech and the song circumscribe a completed unit of emotion and the forms which embody it, and as such it is one of the purest expressions of the Romantic genius in nineteenth century literature. The first line of the song's last stanza recalls, of course, Coleridge's famous "caverns measureless to man," but on reading the entire passage, the impulse is to remark how Poesque it is, how gently it enters and then deeply penetrates the world that lives behind the conscious mind and eye; there it discloses as the song is sung the center of the world so persistently sought by the Romantic imagination, the heart of reality within the dream.

Beddoes' characteristic imagery in the song, its dragon's wing and its fish-lizard were of the world as Pythagoras saw it, and did not anticipate, as Dr. Donner justly observes, the themes of nineteenth century evolution. But Beddoes' visual imagery has still another field of association and in that field strikes deeply at the roots of a mythology which has its being in continental Europe; his Satanism whenever it appears takes on the character of Pieter Brueghel's canvasses; and in reading the lyrical interludes of *Death's Jest-Book*, one carries the images of Brueghel's *The Triumph of Death* and *The Fall of the Rebel Angels* before the eye—and it is that aspect of reality which is perceived and brought to life beneath the surface of the modern world.

Beddoes' power to reawaken the images of Gothic heritage has its own force today; and in Poe's words, the death that looks gigantically down, stares with peculiar intensity upon the map of twentieth century Europe. Now covered with the pall of rearmored warfare, one may perceive in the center of that map, the diminished figure of Beddoes' great Fool, Mandrake, and if one listens one may hear a few lines from a stanza of his song; the scene is lit only by flares dropped from the sky; death's triumph lingers there through broken streets and hallways, and human terror resumes its mask of Gothic irony:

60

Folly hath now turned out of door
Mankind and Fate, who were before
  Jove's Harlequin and Clown.
The world's no stage, no tavern more,
  Its sign, the Fool's ta'en down.

ON EDGAR POE: A BELATED EPITAPH

FIRST of all, so far as the public is concerned, Edgar Poe is in no need of discovery or revival; anthologists of American literature devote a considerable allotment of their treasured "space" to an adequate representation of his prose or verse. And as if to justify the anthologist's concern for Poe's general reputation, four generations of thoroughly respectable Americans have read his *Tales of Mystery and Imagination* with undiminishing, and perhaps (to judge by the number of popular reprint libraries that list among their titles one or another of his books)—no, certainly, increasing enthusiasm. It can be safely said that the works of Edgar Poe are better known (in the wholly selfish sense of being read for pleasure) than the poetry of Longfellow or of Whitman or the novels of Hawthorne, Melville, and Henry James. In contrast to this picture, only the critical attitude seems ill at ease, and of recent years it has been insisting, though almost in a voiceless gesture, that Poe is not to be considered a true poet, that by some sleight of hand or eye or psychic deformity he had tricked us into believing that he was something other than he was.

It is not without reason that critical opinion regards Poe warily, because, as all of us know well—and some of us within the past two decades have learned with grief—that matters of taste, esthetics, morality, religion, and politics cannot come to rest, and indeed, remain unsettled by measuring the fluctuations of popular response. In the case of

Poe, critical objection carries with it a number of highly unpleasant names and it is well to consider a few of them before we go much further. Even the most casual reader of Poe's tales and verse has a word to offer here, and Poe's writings are frequently described as "morbid," "unreal," "unhealthy," or "fanciful." Once the spell of Poe's charm is broken the more attentive and sophisticated reader offers similar objections, and phrases like those of "Romantic Decadence" and "a will toward death" are spoken and repeated. If we ignore the centrifugal powers of Poe's attraction, surely enough *The Fall of the House of Usher* can be made to fit neatly within the bounds of a decidedly unhealthy set of terms—and here even the word, "morbid," would seem to understate the emotions roused by the presence of the lady Madeline of Usher entering the room with blood upon her shroud.

As we reread Poe at his second and third best—and here I am thinking of his vastly overrated poems, *The Raven*, and *The Bells* as well as such pieces in prose as *The Balloon Hoax*, his critical essay, *The Rationale of Verse*, and his burlesques, *The Business Man* and *Diddling Considered as One of the Exact Sciences*, criticism becomes progressively more serious and valid. We should confess that Poe dissipated the atmosphere of what he conceived to be his major poem by an attempt at a grim joke, a very parody of the emotion that shocked his readers into attention of all he had to say:

Then this ebony bird beguiling my sad fancy into smiling,
By the grave and stern decorum of the countenance it wore,
"Though thy crest be shorn and shaven, thou," I said, "art
    sure no craven,
Ghastly grim and ancient Raven wandering from the
    Nightly shore—

Tell me what thy lordly name is on the Night's Plutonian
   shore!
         Quoth the Raven, "Nevermore."

This was the Poe whom Emerson once dismissed as "the
jingle man," the same Poe who defended his skills and
paraded his learning in *The Rationale of Verse*. In his essay
(and not unlike our contemporary, Ezra Pound) he attempted to disarm his enemies, the schoolmasters, by a
superior show of pedantry—and this effort, as we know too
well, was unsuccessful. On this level he contrived *The
Bells* and the sensational report, brilliantly written for the
New York *Sun*, of a balloon that had crossed the Atlantic
westward in three days and landed on the shores of Charles-
ton, South Carolina. This was by no means a disgraceful
second best; and if it was admittedly shallow, and often
meretricious as it entered the field of critical journalism,
it was lively and sharp, intelligent and clear.

As one descends through all the phases of Poe's writing
that were less than his best (and these include the complimentary pieces, his valentines, his *An Enigma*, his second
poem addressed *To Helen*, who this time was the fashionable poetess, Mrs. Whitman), it should be said plainly that
Poe was more frequently the master of artifice than of art.
His conscious skills are all too self-evident and are as
strained as though they were making a desperate reach toward a world of daylight and of sanity. There were moments when he could and did write badly, but in these instances it is as difficult to charge Poe of mediocrity as it is
to defend his exhibitions of childishly defective morality
and taste. At the very heart of his defects, the preternaturally clear view of childhood fears remains one proof of
the "genius" he undoubtedly possessed.

But before we find true glimpses of the genius which

Poe claimed as his own, some attention should be given to the histrionic ability with which he presented his more felicitous ventures into literary criticism. There is an air of neatness, of shabby gentility, conscious of its white collar and clean cuffs surrounding Poe (a fact which his biographers never fail to notice) and which makes its presence felt in his lecture on *The Poetic Principle*. It can be said that the lecture itself resembled a series of delicately timed dramatic entrances and scenes, each bringing to a close its moment of suspense by the recitation of an unfamiliar piece of verse. The small anthology within the lecture was one (so Poe admitted) that suited his own taste and with this preliminary hint of something about to happen, Poe contrived to make the lyrical verses of Shelley, Willis, Longfellow, Bryant, Pinkney, Moore, Hood, Byron, Tennyson, and Motherwell sound very like his own. Between the silent pauses of surprise—and perhaps an approving handclap from his audience—one almost hears Poe's *apologie pour ma vie:* one listens to his remarks on the critics of the *North American Review,* that "magnanimous cabal" which encircled Boston, "the little Athens" of the mid-nineteenth century, one waits to hear the next entry in the charge of dullness against them and when suddenly one catches the name of Coleridge, it is remembered that Poe was among the first in America to read the *Biographia Literaria* with conscious respect. From then onward, the lecturer speaks of the "elevation of the soul" and the "excitement of the heart" through the reading of lyric poetry, and though I suspect that Poe's eloquent use of such passionately abstract terms bewildered the ladies and their gentlemen who heard them, I am nearly certain that his utterance flattered their ability to understand and to applaud him. He had charmed them at the opening of his lecture by the promise that he had no design to be either thorough or profound, but before he stepped down from the platform he had pursued an able course against "size" and "bulk" in poetry, and in general, against "the curse of bigness," which even today—and many times within the past twenty years—has found its echoes in criticism of American life.

Though it may seem a willful paradox to read any moral implications whatsoever in Poe's critical commentaries, yet something that has the sound and color of literary morality has a voice among them—and it is heard even as he satirizes moral judgment of poetic merit in *The Poetic Principle*. In speaking for himself and for the position of the poet in a world where commercial enterprise received an overwhelming share of its own approval and material goods which was the very world of Philadelphia and New York, the slight, yet piercing moral overtone is felt; and like the shrill cry of a bat, it is all too clear once it has been discerned. Poe's list of mock virtues for the scarcely human creatures who practice diddling in *Diddling Considered as One of the Exact Sciences* includes Interest, Perseverance, Ingenuity, Audacity, Nonchalance, Impertinence, and Grin; and these virtues are so defined as to clothe some few of the literary figures of Poe's day as well as "the banker *in petto*" or the small merchant. The essay itself is far too highly pitched, too nervous, too grotesque to be entirely convincing, and in reading it one suffers the same chill of rejection that one experiences in viewing the habits of Dean Swift's Yahoos. Yet the mock virtues as Poe stated them reveal an important aspect of his critical intelligence; one begins to share the sight of evil which Baudelaire perceived at the very center of Poe's active imagination, and we quickly recognize that the same intelligence which Poe employed in his burlesques of *The Business Man's* morality appears in all his comments relating his adventures among

66

the New York literati to his own standards of literary excellence. In *The Mystery of Marie Roget* his experiences in journalism found their reflection in the following passage, which even today requires no further elaboration:

We should bear in mind that, in general, it is the object of our newspapers rather to create a sensation—to make a point— than to further the cause of truth. The latter end is only pursued when it seems coincident with the former.

And in *The Purloined Letter* it is certainly plain that one object of Poe's satire within the story was and still is human stupidity in the person of the Prefect of Police; one sees the satire rise to a small climax as the Prefect betrays his own mental inactivity by ridiculing poetic insight and intelligence, and if one were to translate the Prefect's indolence into moral terms one would find him the very image of sloth and groundless pride.

One need not labor the point that Poe's critical position was heretical, or that in writing his prose narratives and verse, he never failed to follow his own advice. His failures may be obvious enough, failures of taste, proportion, and adult responsibility, but with the possible exception of his essay on *The Rationale of Verse*, he is never dull—and it would be a rare phenomenon indeed to find a reader who had fallen asleep in the progress of following the plot of one of Poe's tales.

It may be said that many of Poe's objects of satire were unworthy of his skill—but so were Alexander Pope's (and we may quote *The Dunciad* to prove it)—yet how cleverly and with sound judgment he discriminated in separating literary sheep from goats, herding the first, his "magnanimous cabal" of the *North American Review* into one field, and the latter, those who were subtly influenced by the mock virtues of diddling into the other:

67

The most "popular," the most "successful" writers among us (for a brief period, at least) are ninety-nine times out of a hundred, persons of mere address, perseverance, effrontery—in a word, busy-bodies, toadies, quacks. These people easily succeed in *boring* editors (whose attention is too often entirely engrossed by politics or other "business" matter) into the admission of favorable notices written or caused to be written by interested parties—or, at least, into the admission of *some* notice where, under ordinary circumstances, *no* notice would be given at all. In this way ephemeral "reputations" are manufactured which, for the most part, serve all the purposes designated—that is to say, the putting of money into the purse of the quack and the quack's publisher; for there never was a quack who could be brought to comprehend the value of mere fame. Now, men of genius will not resort to these manoeuvers. . . .

The paradox of Poe's morality as he applied it to the writers of his time may be reread today with little loss of pertinancy or freshness; and it is only when we hear him bringing charges of plagiarism against Longfellow that we re-encounter the darkened atmosphere in which the figure of Poe is the injured and yet petted child of an indulgent foster mother.

As we return to the prospect of a world that Poe saw in his childhood we rediscover the vividness of his attraction for the common reader. Poe's appeal is to the private world that exists in all of us, the world that Mr. E. M. Forster has so aptly described as the true "Ivory Tower," and which has always been the necessary and common refuge of the social human being whenever he seeks self-knowledge and wishes to be alone. Poe intensified the realization of that necessary refuge by the detailed descriptions of "being cast adrift" in *The Narrative of A. Gordon Pym* and throughout the course of telling that remarkable story, Poe touches depths of psychological reality that have been distorted or ignored by those who have attempted to explain his character by a facile use of Freudian analysis. The same penetration into the private world of human experience may be discerned in the following lines which were posthumously printed in 1875 and have not received the attention they deserve:

> From childhood's hour I have not been
> As others were; I have not seen
> As others saw; I could not bring
> My passions from a common spring.
> From the same source I have not taken
> My sorrow; I could not awaken
> My heart to joy at the same tone;
> And all I loved, *I* loved alone.
> Then—in my childhood, in the dawn
> Of a most stormy life—was drawn
> From every depth of good and ill
> The mystery which binds me still:
> From the torrent, or the fountain,
> From the red cliff of the mountain,
> From the sun that round me rolled
> In its autumn tint of gold,
> From the lightning in the sky
> As it passed me flying by,
> From the thunder and the storm,
> And the cloud that took the form
> (When the rest of Heaven was blue)
> Of a demon in my view.

Aside from the autobiographical nature of the poem what it has to say touches upon an experience common to self-identity in adolescence, the secret confession that the individual stands alone, victorious perhaps, in feeling himself distinct from all other creatures of God's making, but burdened with the self-love-and-pity of Narcissus. From this last extremity Poe frees himself (and the impressionable reader) by the image of a "demon" in his view; and the "demon" in its excellent ambiguity may be a figure of genius or a sight of evil, but probably signifies the two-in-one in a single look directed up toward Heaven.

The "demon" is, of course, Poe's close familiar, and its appearance in the poem describes the shifting of the newly awakened ego from the pride of seeming singular and distinct to pride of being among the fallen and outcast angels. This salvation from the fate of the too-beautiful Narcissus is not merely the mutation of a sensibility in Romantic literature, but it exists and endures within all poetry that expresses the fullness and release of youthful emotion; it is the obverse side of the same coin which presents its self-identity to God, or to Nature, or to an amorphous vision of mankind, or to a concept (as Shelley saw it) of Platonic love.

Surely the circumstances of Poe's life nourished and enlarged the internal conviction that he occupied a unique position in the world. One might almost say that his marriage to Virginia Clemm (including his adoption of Virginia's mother as his own) was a decision which carried childhood with him into middle age, and indeed, within two years of his own death. In reading Poe, the childhood visit to England with its sight of Gothic towers and its glimpse of the sea's terrors during the long Atlantic voyage should not be ignored; here one restores fragments of Poe's memory which seem to float irresistibly to the surfaces of his shorter poems. One sees them in his "ultimate dim Thule," his "bottomless vales and boundless floods," his "Time-eaten towers that tremble not," his "o'er the Past (Dim gulf!) my spirit hovering," and brilliantly, his "one bright island smile." If these memories were brought to consciousness through his readings in the poetry of his day, or reinspired through his experiments in taking drugs, their actual sources and their "sepulchre by the sea" are definitely circumscribed by the first fourteen years of his life.

No poet (and indeed Wordsworth's recollections of childhood seem positively remote compared to these) has expressed the scenes of terror within childhood's fears with more enduring vividness than Poe; Rainer Maria Rilke's *Kindheit* with its "*kleine bleiche Gesicht, das sinkend aus dem Teiche schien*" has, I admit, far more delicacy of perception into the same complex of youthful desires and an adult sense of loss, but Poe holds his own by associating a lack of security (which is so often felt and realized by the sensitive and unhappy child) with the conviction of being prematurely doomed, of being predestined for madness or for Hell.

In this sense, Poe's position in American literature during the first half of the nineteenth century is one that seems to stand alone; and if as critic he performed the same services in opposing dull-witted authority in the United States that Lewis Carroll voiced through Alice's lips during her adventures through wonderland and the looking-glass in Victorian England, his situation as a poet was no less critical, and in the worldly gaze of rival critics no less untenable. Poe, like the then unknown Thomas Lovell Beddoes and not unlike the youthful Longfellow and Tennyson, was a belated arrival on the Romantic scene. In America, Longfellow's relationship to his European contemporaries seemed more tangible, and even more "official" than any claim that Poe might have had to offer. While Longfellow traveled through Germany, Italy, and Spain in search of a soul that came to rest at Harvard and received the Smith professorship in comparative literatures, Poe's contact with the Europe of that day was limited to the reading of British periodicals that drifted through John Allan's commercial importing house in Richmond. As Longfellow's travels increased his reputation as an interpreter of modern Europe to Harvard undergraduates, Poe's readings in European letters—however intensive they were or seemed to be—were broadened only by his duties in editorial offices or by the writing of book reviews. Probably the fact that the latter half of his education was conduced in public tended to diminish what little respect he might have earned among the leaders of Boston's intellectual elite; certainly his disastrous experiences at the University of Virginia and at West Point were not of a nature to excite sympathy or understanding in the benign circle of gifted men who had confessed their allegiance to New England soil and were never weary of acknowledging the debt of their educational heritage to Harvard. Viewed in their perspective the singularity of Poe's poetry was heightened by its infrequency of classical image and reference; and today as then, his glory that was Greece and the grandeur that was Rome must be perceived through colors that are stained by the green tides of the city in sea or the Gothic fire of the Palace Metzengerstein. If at extremely infrequent intervals his classical images seem to shed or to reflect a purer light, it is of Psyche who is out of favor with her lover, or of the sexless, sky-wandering Aphrodite. We may, I think, allow a moment of speculation to enter here, and admit that a probable origin of Poe's angels and feminine deities floated in his imagination against the painted and domed ceiling of a church which he visited in early childhood in Richmond, safely escorted by his foster-parents. But for us, it is perhaps more important to realize that his imagination had created its world at an immeasurable distance from the Colonial classicism of Jefferson and of New England. In this particular Poe's relationship to an American culture will always seem extraordinary; and in general, our literary and historical imagination looks backward through the neoclassic eighteenth century to an Athens that never existed on our soil, and when it attempts to gaze into the future, it dimly discerns with growing optimism, the seemingly endless cycles of rebirth. In this climate, or atmosphere, or whatever name we wish to call it, the phenomenon of Edgar Poe is all too likely to appear as an anomaly—and so it does until we remember that its emotional associations are of the secret places of the heart, and that they touch the springs of human failure. In this latter view it is significant that Paul Elmer More perceived a relationship that existed between Poe and Hawthorne, and here Poe's lonely figure stands at a not too distant call from the Herman Melville who wrote *Pierre* and the unread *Poems*, and in our day, it is not impossibly remote from the E. A. Robinson who conceived the spiritual isolation of *The Man Who Died Twice*. And perhaps —although it is still too soon to say that a similar critical uneasiness will result—we may yet discover that the exile of Poe in Baltimore, Philadelphia, or in New York was a shadowy premonition of Ezra Pound's exile in Italy.

In America no poet so widely read as Poe has left behind him so small a number of poems on which to rest the usual vicissitudes of fame. By a generous count and including the fragmentary *Politian*, the youthful and experimental *Al Aaraaf* and *Tamberlane*, the number rises to a scant half-hundred. After his second and third best poems have been dismissed, the number that remain are incredibly small, but among these few, Poe's imagination illuminates a world that has enduring relationship to the myths and *Popular Stories* of MM. Grimm (which, by the way, had been translated into English with revelatory notes and commentaries in

1823 and in 1826). In *The Sleeper*, and in *Romance*, and in *Lenore*, it is as though Poe had reached the same depths of delight and of terror that are perceived where the sun and moon and the night wind speak their warnings, where Rose-Bud sleeps her many years (is it sleep or death?) within an enchanted forest. In Poe's verses, no Prince escapes the spell, and the rescuing figure is powerless to disenchant the scene:

> Far in the forest, dim and old,
> For her may some tall vault unfold
> Against whose sounding door she hath thrown,
> In childhood, many an idle stone—
> Some tomb, which oft hath flung its black
> And vampire-winged panels back,
> Flutt'ring triumphant o'er the palls
> Of her old family funerals.

Poe's spell-encircled Princesses are of the same ancient lineage that speaks in *"Van den Machandel-Boom"*:

> *Min Moder de mi slacht't*
> *Min Vader de mi att,*
> *Min Swester de Marleeniken*
> *Socht alle mine Beeniken,*
> *Un bindt se in een syden Dook,*
> *Legts unner den Machandel-boom.*
> *Kywitt! Kywitt! ach watt een schon Vagel bin ick!*

It is when one is certain that Poe freed himself from the conscious skills that he practiced so diligently in *The Raven* and in *The Bells* that one hears the accents that have assured him of an immortality; in *To One in Paradise*, the vision is restored of what Grimm's soldier saw as he witnessed, wrapped in his cloak of invisibility, the secret places where the twelve dancing Princesses held midnight festival:

74

> And all my days are trances,
>   And all my nightly dreams
> Are where thy grey eye glances,
>   And where thy footstep gleams—
> In what ethereal dances,
>   By what eternal streams.

To this order of Poe's imagination I also attribute the first of his poems bearing the title *To Helen* and *The City in the Sea;* they are of a quality that one discovers in an imagination that glances the roots of human evil and super-human joy, and reveals their existence among the fears and desires of childhood origin. The "truth" of which Poe spoke so often in his critical asides was a truth that illuminated the hidden chambers of the human psyche, and among his fellows whom he saw on the streets of Philadelphia and of New York, his discovery, as he looked inward to the sources of his own spirit, was of the darkened, private aspect of the multitudinous cheerful face that met its clients and its creditors, its friends at a card table or at a game of draughts. Within that multitude of faces, hardened by what he called the "Grin," his personal appearance was obviously singular, and for a brief time he exerted the full dexterity of his intelligence to take advantage of what seemed to be a singular position in the world about him.

Perhaps Edgar Poe will always remain an embarrassment in critical discussions of American literature; and, of course, the final word that reilluminates completely the world of his imagination cannot and will never be written by a hand other than his own. For my part, I would repeat his warning which should be remembered as his epitaph: "The terror of which I write is not of Germany but of the soul."

75

ON WALTER SAVAGE LANDOR AND THE
ELEGIAC TRADITION IN ENGLISH POETRY

> I know what wages beauty gives,
> How hard a life her servant lives,
> Yet praise the winters gone:
> There is not a fool can call me friend,
> And I may dine at journey's end
> With Landor and with Donne.

AS one rereads the last line of Yeats's poem which appears so archly placed under the title, *To a Young Beauty*, it is natural to ask why Landor's name is there. We should agree that Yeats wished to be seated in the rarest company, and in keeping with twentieth century taste, it is signified by the presence of John Donne, but Landor is so clearly unlike Donne that the choice makes for strange companionship at dinner. I am not prepared to think of what Donne and Landor would have to say to one another; that is a problem that Yeats, having passed his journey's end, must solve,—yet in one respect, Yeats was intuitively right: Landor's poetry at its best is among the rarities of our present heritage, and it enjoys, even today, an almost esoteric fame.

The poetry of Walter Savage Landor has the dubious distinction of being known chiefly through the helpful intentions of those who compile anthologies of English verse, and through their offices, its album pieces and scattered epigrams have suffered tedious repetition. It is not that the selections to which I refer have preserved Landor for us at his worst, but that repetition through the wear of time have made the few choice quotations seem thin and bodiless. In that light one thinks of it as possessing the qualities of finely tempered and beautifully wrought costume jewelry, and in reading it, an impression is left of graceful compliments being paid to ladies and of the author's readiness to depart from the sinking fire of life. These qualities, which include the merits of seeming cool and chaste and firm are deceptively easy to admire and then to set aside: "I strove with none," "the fire sinks," and that (it is very easy to conclude) is all that Landor had to say.

The many years of Landor's life, from 1775 to 1864, endowed him with an unusual richness of contemporaries. In Landor's youth George Crabbe was vigorously alive (with Jane Austen among his most discriminating admirers) —and the Pre-Raphaelites never forgot Swinburne's greetings to Landor as "England's eldest singer." Yet Landor's position had the superficial character of seeming to fall outside the literary movements of his day. His radical Toryism was, of course, enough to disenchant him in the eyes of Leigh Hunt's circle; Landor had seen Napoleon in the flesh at arm's length and did not share Byron's disillusion in hero-worship; he was as far removed from Wordsworth as from the youthful eloquence of Keats—and in his poetry it can be said that he lived through his age without falling to rest within it.

In his personal conduct (which has been the concern of his biographers from John Foster to Malcolm Elwin) his eccentricities, his years of self-imposed exile in Italy, his restlessness, his mismanagement of even the most casual of his domestic affairs follow the general pattern of misfortunes which attended the careers of Coleridge, Shelley, and Byron; in his narratives and dramatic sketches not a few of his subjects and scenes are as "Romantic" as anyone could well desire; in these, he enjoyed the same interests that were shared by such temperamental opposites as Southey and Byron, but his occupation with classical themes and his sustained respect for traditional verse forms make it extremely difficult to speak too seriously of his "Romantic behavior" and its consequences.

In contrast to a number of young men who wrote poetry in his day, Landor was not precocious. His early writings contained little of the youthful brilliance that won partisans for the authors of *The Lyrical Ballads, Childe Harold, The Brides' Tragedy, Endymion,* and *Adonais;* Southey admired Landor's *Gebir,* but it must be confessed that *Gebir,* as well as the majority of his *Heroic Idylls,* belongs to that unhappy company of highly praised and industrious works of literature which include at one end of the spectrum Moore's *Lalla Rookh,* and at the other, Matthew Arnold's *Sohrab and Rustum.* Briefly, they are dull, and it requires greater industry to reread them than the effort that had been spent in creating their histrionic episodes and gestures.

There has been a tradition (which still exists in English literature) to measure a poet's stature by his ability to write a long narrative poem, rhymed or unrhymed, a poem, which as time goes on, has less resemblance to the ancient epic than to something described in publishers' announcements as "a novel in verse." Since Milton's day the successful composition of a narrative poem which runs beyond six hundred lines has become increasingly rare. Pope's translation of Homer may be counted an exception, and so may the realistic chronicles of George Crabbe; Byron's mock epic, *Don Juan,* is still another, and Longfellow's *Tales of a Wayside Inn,* remain as lively as on the first day

78

of their publication. Since 1900, E. A. Robinson's narratives may be looked upon as further exceptions to the rule —but are they? They are both more meditative and more dramatic in character than what is usually accepted when we think of narrative verse; their closest parallels are to be found in Crabbe's chronicles of the Borough and the Parish Register; and of Robinson Jeffers' tales in verse (in which another exception can be brought up for the sake of argument) the best of them, *The Tower Beyond Tragedy*, closely approximates dramatic form.

However popular they may have been, however impressive they may have seemed at the moment of their arrival, narratives in verse resemble the character of fool's gold, and almost without exception they suffer the tarnish and destruction that time bestows upon a work whose ambitious intentions outride the excellence of its performance. Even as one generation of readers buys the latest attempt to emulate Homer, or Alexander Pope, or Milton, it yawns and falls asleep over an effort of the same kind which had the temerity to be written twenty-five or fifty years ago. At best, the modern narrative in verse yields a number of briefly inspired and isolated passages which may be quoted to prove the existence of a gifted writer, and it is charitable to view them in the same light that one finds interest in the studio paintings (many of which have been discarded by their maker) of a famous artist.

It is for this last reason only that Landor's narratives in verse deserve attention—and I must confess that the interest is more necrological, and, perhaps, more academic, than it is inspiring. Through reading them one seems to enter into the secrets of his writing table: one learns of his experiments in blank verse, of his writing some passages in Latin before presenting them in English, of his wide familiarity with the literature of Plutarch, Gibbon, Virgil, Dante, and

Tasso, of his habits of hasty reading and rapid composition —but the poems are less poems in themselves.than they are the fruit of Landor's enthusiasms in making literary discoveries, and of his speculating with heated vehemence upon them.

In the majority of his historical romances in verse and in his plays, Landor seems to impose his willful fancies upon his characters; his *Gebir,* his *Count Julian,* his elderly *Ulysses* are all presented without the benefit of psychological motivation. All are larger than life-size and are as wooden, though by no means as impressive, as the Etruscan gods and heroes who stand guard within the walls of the Metropolitan Museum—and by comparison, even the Etruscan warriors seem to possess an image of life held within an eternal stillness that Landor's heroes lack. By their very nature the Etruscan gods inspire awe through silence, while Landor's heroes deliver their opinions in the language of poetic discourse, speaking what could have been better and more tersely said within the pages of a book of critical essays.

But perhaps the greatest barrier, the thickest walls of print, that stand between the world and the best of Landor's poetry are his own works in prose, the *Imaginary Conversations,* which so completely overshadowed his reputation as a poet, and so hugely instructed and entertained their readers in those moments which were reserved for leisure by our grandfathers. Landor was equally delighted by their success, for praise and fame were brought to his doors through publication of a novelty in English letters. The novelty was something that gave the illusion of being both a one-act play and a short-story, and yet was neither —nor was it quite a Platonic dialogue or a literary essay— but it seemed to combine the merits of all four media, and the little sketches could be read aloud in the drawing room as though the speaker were reciting the most intimate of closet dramas for the entertainment of his guests, or the instruction of his wife, or son, or daughter. Great names and characters made rhetorical entrances and exits from the page—one had the pleasure of hearing that one was face to face with Oliver Cromwell, or Catherine of Russia, or Hannibal, or Diogenes, or Plato, or Marcellus. In effect, the appeal (and unreality) of their appearance was not at all unlike many of the present experiments in radio drama, and Landor welcomed the task of writing his *Imaginary Conversations* with a nearly professional eye; he had conceived a means of expressing his political ideas, his concepts of history, his literary opinions to the British public—did it matter that his fanciful conversation between Horace and Virgil was actually lifeless and devoid of wit? Not in the least; it had the air of conveying information, and the best-known facts were seldom violated. His characters possessed everything but an enduring vitality: they were capable of thought and violent action; they pleaded and declaimed; they declared undying love or hatred for one another—yet the flexible rhetoric in which they spoke weaves and rambles monotonously up and down and across the page. Did the classical dialogues of the *Imaginary Conversations* anticipate the prose which later ripened into the sinuous withdrawals and embraces of Walter Pater's *Marius the Epicurean?* I suspect they did, and despite their tendency to ramble from whatever had been chosen as the subject of a prolonged discussion, Landor's speech flows from a source of greater purity and firmness of expression than can be found in any comparable passage of Pater's prose. Landor's biographers accent, justly enough, the consistent and deeply unfortunate nature of his unworldliness, of his unhappy fortunes in dealing with his wife and children, of his misadventures in his attempts to be a landlord—the same lack of insight pervades the atmosphere of his *Imaginary Conversations*. They provided relaxation for the eager-to-be-well-read Victorian; all the delights of historical fancy and memory were rediscovered in their pages, but the breath of life was noted only by its absence.

If Landor lacked the knowledge of human character other than his own, what he did possess was an inspired apppreciation of a Graeco-Roman heritage in literature, but the true expression of its spirit in his own verse waited upon the arrival of his maturity. It can be said fairly that he did not begin to write poetry until he was past fifty, and then how brilliant, how clear, how firm are his *Hellenics!* And if one contrasts them with the lines of Keats's *Hyperion*, one reads the difference between the patient, conscious artistry of youthful talent and the easy strength of a mature poet who had found his tongue and could speak aloud without the merest sign of effort.

It can be said that the *Hellenics* introduce the reader to the hundred poems and more which comprise the rarities of Landor's gifts and from which the anthologists have made their selection. In the *Hellenics* (and I refer particularly to *The Hamadryad* and *Iphigeneia*) the figures of youthful love and sacrifice are graced with a purity of color and movement that is seldom equaled and almost never surpassed in English poetry. In these brief narratives one does not ask for, nor does one feel the lack of psychological subtlety and conflict, and an illustration of what I mean is presented in the closing lines of *Iphigeneia:*

> She lookt up and saw
> The fillet of the priest and calm cold eyes.
> Then turn'd she where her parent stood, and cried
> "O father! grieve no more: the ships can sail."

It is here that the purity of Landor's speech is clearly heard, but in saying so I realize that as one speaks of purity in poetry, a word of explanation is required.

The search for whatever is called "pure" in poetry usually defeats its purpose in the rediscovery of minor lyric verse; and, because of this, we had best, I think, confine our attention to that quality of expression which is found in the writings of Ben Jonson, but is absent from Chapman's *Homer*—that quality which makes its presence known in the verses of John Wilmot, Earl of Rochester—and which must be sought for with only the briefest intervals of reward in the poetry of the seventeenth century "metaphysicals." It is readily discoverable in Dryden's prose and almost totally absent from the pages of Sir Thomas Browne's *Urn Burial*. Its expression, when we find it, is a first cousin of what Shakespeare named as "simple truth" and which was so unhappily miscalled "simplicity."

The simple truth, so hard to come by anywhere, implies, of course, a lucid statement of it, and however unforced its accomplishment may be, it is almost never as simple as it seems. Wordsworth, I fear, often confused it with the unbrilliant simplicity that Shakespeare so rightly and so cleverly rejected. I believe that in poetry the presence of simple truth and the pure expression of it, cannot be called into being by anything less than art, nor can it be conjured out of a vacuum by an act of will.

In his later poems Landor relinquished the power of conscious will and the poetic ambitions of his early narratives in verse. The public success of his *Imaginary Conversations* had released him from the bitterness and the internal distractions of seeming to be forgotten while younger men received the highest praise. As he wrote to Robert Browning in 1831, the *Conversations* were his "business"; and like Byron, he preferred to think of himself as an English gentleman, freed from the necessity of ever writing a line of poetry at all—except when the internal, impulsive moment of necessity arrived. Perhaps this attitude was no more than a restatement of Congreve's desire to be known as a gentleman rather than the author of *The Way of the World*, but in Landor one perceives it as an admirable defense of his easily wounded and abrasive ego. It was an attitude that Yeats sought in part to emulate and to revive —which was to be a poet only through the demands of an inner being and compulsion, and not through the external circumstances of good fortune or bad, or to be dependent upon the mutations of poetic fame.

It was the Landor of the love lyrics, the brief elegies, the poet who had outlived deservedly famous and younger men, and it was he with whom Yeats wished to dine at journey's end. For twenty years Landor wrote each poem as though it were his last, and as their number increases, their scope and variety almost equals the multitudinous, bell-tolling stanzas of Tennyson's *In Memoriam*. If it is possible to say that almost every poem, every translation that Samuel Johnson wrote was devotional in spirit, in the same fashion almost every lyric that Landor set down on paper, irrespective of whether or not it was addressed to Rose Aylmer or to Lady Blessington or to "Ianthe," was a revival of the elegiac note in English poetry. Here, Landor's mastery is unmistakably complete, and here, it is true enough that he "strove with none." Within them Landor spoke in the language of the unforced, seemingly inevitable phrase which bears so close a resemblance to the statement of "simple truth," and which Yeats in his middle years so consciously admired. The mastery of such an art is very like the discovery of finding "freedom within form," which should always be the last reward of a lifetime spent in the writing of poetry. One hears its accents with its elegiac undertones in

> Rose Aylmer, whom these wakeful eyes
>   May weep, but never see,
> A night of memories and of sighs
>   I consecrate to thee.

And in Yeats, and in, of course, his own emotional environment, the same spirit is revived, the same notes are struck:

> When day begins to break
> I count my good and bad,
> Being wakeful for her sake,
> Remembering what she had,
> What eagle look still shows,
> While up from my heart's root
> So great a sweetness flows
> I shake from head to foot.

As one reads further into Landor's shorter poems, the distance between his time and ours seems to diminish, and that happy illusion is of the same character that makes certain passages of Dryden's *All for Love*, and a half-dozen of Rochester's lyrics seem as fresh as though they were written yesterday. Admitting that we are living in an age that is highly appreciative of an elegiac spirit in poetry, and that young men and their elders have been saying farewell repeatedly to the generation which preceded theirs, it is not this sentiment alone that endows the large majority of Landor's shorter pieces with a quality which remains unaffected by the distance in time between our day and his. We are refreshed by a language which seems "modern" in a sense that the poetry of many of Landor's contemporaries does not—the speech is direct and less consciously poetic (to the reader's ear at least) than, let us say, the language of *Adonais* or of *Endymion*. In his remarks on "age," does Landor's speech seem more remote than that of Yeats or of Housman?

> Death, tho I see him not, is near
> And grudges me my eightieth year.
> Now, I would give him all these last
> For one that fifty have run past.
> Ah! he strikes all things, all alike,
> But bargains: those he will not strike.

But for the exception of the presence of "beauteous" the following lines under the uninviting title *On Hair Falling Off After an Illness*, might well have been written during the last twenty years:

> Conon was he whose piercing eyes
> Saw Berenice's hair surmount the skies,
> Saw Venus spring away from Mars
> And twirl it round and fix it 'mid the stars.
> Then every poet who had seen
> The glorious sight sang to the youthful queen,
> Until the many tears were dried,
> Shed for that hair by that most lovely bride.
> Hair far more beauteous be it mine
> Not to behold amid the lights divine,
> But gracing, as it graced before,
> A brow serene which happier men adore.

The same quality of freshness, and I suspect, the same evidence of poetic maturity, is readily perceived in this brief passage among the many written to "Ianthe":

> The torch of Love dispels the gloom
> Of life, and animates the tomb;

But never let it idly flare
On gazers in the open air,
Nor turn it quite away from one
To whom it serves for moon and sun,
And who alike in night or day
Without it could not find his way.

If the *Conversations* were Landor's "business," the writing of his shorter poems filled the moments of his leisure, and he continued to write them in the same fashion that a gentleman of the eighteenth century carried a sword. The poems had become as closely identified with his daily being as his habit of buying canvasses in second-hand shops to hang on the walls of his apartment, or to give away to friends. "My pictures blacken in their frames," he wrote,

As night comes on,
And youthful maids and wrinkled dames
Are now all one.

Death of the day! A sterner death
Did worse before;
The fairest form, the sweetest breath
Away he bore.

That degree of serenity and of self-knowledge which Landor expresses so well and learned so late, places him in the company of those few poets whose gifts outlast the excitements of their youth and survive the triumphs, the humiliations, the self-deceptions, and the glories of false pride which are, too often, the sum of human experiences during middle age. Landor's wisdom was of a sort that was incommunicable in any of his activities except that of writing verse; certainly it was not related to the continued mismanagement of his large income which spared him only the extremes of poverty, nor to his long-sustained quarrels with a number of his relatives. His unworldliness, his impulsive fits of anger and of generosity possessed the charms of youthful innocence; the poise he achieved was in his poetry: there, the world he saw was neither broken nor misinterpreted. How clearly the misadventures of his life are resolved within it, and how brilliantly in *The Casket* his wisdom illuminates what in less gifted writers is merely the darkness of old age!

> Sure, 'tis time to have resign'd
> All the dainties of the mind,
> And to take a little rest
> After Life's too lengthen'd feast.
> Why then turn the casket-key?
> What is there within to see?
> Whose is this dark twisted hair?
> Whose this other, crisp and fair?
> Whose the slender ring? now broken
> Undesignedly, a token,
> Love said *mine;* and Friendship said
> *So I fear;* and shook her head.

The ease of statement and its restraint, the finality of accent, the turn of an excellent conceit—all of which distinguish the mark of a true style in poetry are there. It is what we think of when we attempt to describe those qualities of style which are distinctly separate from the more spectacular and less enduring qualities of a highly seasoned personal mannerism in writing verse. We are not concerned with the poem's originality, but with the authenticity of its expression. It is this quality that the greater number of Landor's shorter poems convey, and their abundance indicates a writer of greater stature than can be brought to light within the pages of an anthology.

Someone among Landor's late contemporaries—his name

is unimportant and has been forgotten—linked Landor's reputation and his artistry with that of Goethe's, a rash comparison which was smiled upon at the time as a flattering and overly enthusiastic compliment; perhaps it was, for we must accept the presence of Landor without a Faust, without a Werther, without a Wilhelm Meister, and without a Weimar and an Eckermann. Yet both men preserved within their writings the formal graces of the century in which they were born, and both lived through an age that first welcomed and then slowly recovered from its period of *Sturm und Drang*. Though Landor did not possess the steadiness of mind and of character that we acknowledge in the existence of Goethe's major works, if we remember the particular qualities of Goethe's lyrics, a comparison of them and their felicities to the later poems of Landor is not totally inept nor unconvincing.

In the failure of his dramatic sketches Landor has a position not far removed from the robust company of Byron and Robert Browning; in the successes of his *Imaginary Conversations* he is of that long list of writers who in each age gratify the tastes of a single generation and leave few traces of their remains behind them; it is only in the excellence of the poems which he wrote without ambition, and with little hope of gaining the attention of posterity, that his reputation has earned the respect and the neglect of isolation. To say that he was not unconscious of his position is an understatement, for in his last years, an awareness of its singularity had become the source of the remaining vestige of his pride; and if the world has been slow to recognize the true and enduring merits that were his, surely the voice of his shade in whatever world it may inhabit would be the last voice heard to speak in accents of disappointment or complaint.

ON LEWIS CARROLL'S ALICE AND HER WHITE

KNIGHT AND WORDSWORTH'S *ODE* ON

IMMORTALITY

What though the radiance which was once so bright
Be now for ever taken from my sight,
  Though nothing can bring back the hour
Of splendour in the grass, of glory in the flower;
    We will grieve not, rather find
    Strength in what remains behind;
    In the primal sympathy
    Which having been must ever be . . .

> —Stanza X, *Ode Intimations of
> Immortality from Recollec-
> tions of Early Childhood.*

"Then you keep moving round, I suppose?" said Alice.

"Exactly so," said the Hatter: "as the things get used up."

"But what happens when you come to the beginning again?"
Alice ventured to ask.

"Suppose we change the subject," the March Hare interrupted, yawning. "I'm getting tired of this. I vote the young
lady tells us a story."

"I'm afraid I don't know one," said Alice, rather alarmed
at the proposal.

"Then the Dormouse shall!" they both cried. "Wake up,
Dormouse!"

> —Chapter VII, "A Mad Tea-Party,"
> *Alice's Adventures in Wonderland.*

It is in like manner and with no intentional disrespect to literature itself, that each generation from Pindar's day to this changes the subject slightly and tells its story. I would like to suggest that even the Dormouse's story as it was told on a fine mid-Victorian afternoon is not entirely irrelevant to the subject of Wordsworth's *Ode* on Immortality. We remember that the Dormouse spoke of three sisters who had been living at the bottom of a well (to be exact, it was a treacle well) and that they drew (they had been learning how to draw) all manner of things from it, everything that began with M, such as mouse-trap, and the moon, memory and muchness: and today, as we reread the *Ode*, memory and muchness disturb us most, and from these we progress toward Wordsworth's moon who with delight looked round her when the heavens were bare.

If one rereads the poem for the sake of recapturing the associations it once held, it is likely to contain memories which its long title half-unconsciously revives; and none of us, I think, can hold Wordsworth or the *Ode* wholly responsible for this phenomenon. For most of us the earliest reading of the poem had its beginning in a school classroom, with Wordsworth read (as Alice's Gryphon might well recall) at odd moments between the study of those superior branches of learning which include Ambition, Distraction, Uglification, and Derision. My own recollection of the *Ode* is surrounded by the images of a boys' preparatory school, where, behind a desk, a young, thin, nervous, red-headed Scotchman sat—and it was he who instructed us in English poetry, basketball, and tennis. I remember him reciting Shakespeare and *The Jabberwocky* with a recklessness that matched his leaps and rushes on the concrete tennis-court—and in his reading of Wordsworth's *Ode*, he accented a touch of malice (which all of us shared in the reciting the poets of the Lake School) by a slight exaggeration of his Edinburgh burr: one could hear it clearly as he read aloud:

> Our birth is but a sleep and a forgetting:
> The Soul that rises with us, our life's Star,
>   Hath had elsewhere its setting
>   And cometh from afar . . .

As one heard the *rrs*, the atmosphere increased its tension, for it was part of our unspoken agreement not to laugh aloud at Wordsworth's famous *Ode*. Without knowing why, we felt immensely superior to the image of the lank and gray-haired, long-nosed, elderly poet whose head leaned with a weak, womanish tilt out of the darkness of a photo-plated engraving which faced the title page of Wordsworth's *Poetical Works;* it was an unvoiced pact between us to read him with an air of prep-school skepticism, and to justify our attitude by frequently reciting:

> "O mercy!" to myself I cried,
> "If Lucy should be dead!"

Yet we could not dismiss him utterly; for the *Ode* was almost certain to turn up in awkward places: its title would reappear in questioning footnotes in schoolbook anthologies of English verse and scrawled in chalk upon the classroom blackboard. From a sense of duty to his students (and the power exerted by college entrance boards), our instructor persisted in the revival of the *Ode* on mimeographed sheets of paper that were rapidly circulated around the room during the weighted silence of a moment which always precedes a written examination. Who wrote it and what did the poem mean, and what, O what was Wordsworth's philosophy? This last we agreed, if not completely understood, was called "Pantheism," and was of heavier substance than anything that went by the name of philosophy in the poetry of Shelley, Keats, or Byron, and one could prove it (if I remember correctly) by contrasting two skylark poems in which it was shown that Shelley lost himself in Nature, while Wordsworth, in a trying hour was found. It was agreed that Wordsworth somehow achieved salvation and, if less attractive than Byron or Coleridge, was out of danger—was safe and not to be questioned in open controversy; it was as though Wordsworth's recollections of childhood had begun at the very moment when the pleasures of our own had vanished. From a last reading of his *Ode* one went to college, leaving the memories of *The Solitary Reaper, The Reverie of Poor Susan, To a Skylark, I Travelled Among Unknown Men,* and fragmentary stanzas of *Resolution and Independence,* floating and yet heard distinctly within the recesses of the inner ear.

To speak of Wordsworth and his *Ode* again today is like asking oneself the question that Alice ventured: "But what happens when you come to the beginning again?" So much has happened to Wordsworth and ourselves that a true beginning is difficult to find: one road winds backward to the first decade of the nineteenth century in which the *Ode* was written, another to what we mean when we speak of poetry at all, and still another to Alice herself and to her childhood which was overshadowed by the unnamed presence of Wordsworth among the trees of that dark forest where the White Knight recited his ballad of *The Aged, Aged Man.*

Since I confess a predilection for the second and third of three possible beginnings, I shall speak of the first only as it serves to illuminate the darkness surrounding Alice as "she leant against a tree . . . listening in a half-dream to the melancholy music of the song." The first road recalls a number of familiar images, images of Rousseau and of the Fall of the Bastille, the title page of Blake's *Songs of Innocence*, Mr. Thomas Day's adopted daughter, Sabrina, the educated orphan, whose innate goodness was severely tested by her foster-father ("It is said that he dropped hot sealing wax on her arms to inure her to pain, and fired blank cartridges at her petticoats to train her in self-control."), images of Mr. Day's Sanford and Merton, Miss Maria Edgeworth's Lazy Lawrence, and among them that dark-eyed, semi-tragic child of genius, Hartley Coleridge, of whom it has been so often said that he was the living prototype of the child within the *Ode:*

> Behold the child among his new-born blisses,
> A six years' Darling of a pigmy size!

These and a hundred other pictures crowd the scene, filling a decade of unresolved Napoleonic Wars: Miss Austen's precocious girls with clear heads and cool fingers tripped between them—and everywhere the hope of the world was seen in a child's face, the child no longer stained by sin, the guiltless child, and the innocent, even idiot boy was believed to possess the secret of human happiness. The reflected likeness of that child may be seen in the pallid, soot-streaked features of Smike and Oliver Twist who followed after, and after them, came the pink-cheeked, May-pole dancing figurines of Miss Kate Greenaway; and a distinct resemblance to the child's behavior may be found among the heroes of social novels, ranging their separate ways through the fiction of the twentieth century.

Returning to the *Ode* itself and the moment of its birth, we would agree, I think, that its so-called philosophic generalities had been given the particulars of light, shade, depth, color, and motion in a number of Wordsworth's earlier poems: *Her Eyes Are Wild, We Are Seven, The Sparrow's Nest, The Reverie of Poor Susan, Michael*, and

94

I Travelled Among Unknown Men, were of the same world that was viewed so hopefully in the opening stanzas of the *Ode.* His readers were familiar with its terms; they knew its "Fountains, Meadows, Hills, and Groves," they shared the emotion implied by the use of each abstract noun within the *Ode:* each joy, each grief, each bliss, each soul, each glory; and, I think, we may grant that they were as well prepared to read the poem as he was to write it. Even the difficult concept of human immortality was expressed in a language that Wordsworth's early readers (with the aid of his prefatory note) could accept and welcome, and as they rediscovered it within the *Ode,* it seemed to fall into place as effortlessly as sunlight upon the earth. So much then, for our first beginning, which in itself could be expanded into a volume of considerable size and weight. From what we know of the *Ode* and its predecessors, we are reasonably safe in saying that it summed up a number of the beliefs and observations which had been already exposed to light in eloquent passages of *The Prelude* and which had taken form in the first ten stanzas of *Resolution and Independence.*

Our second beginning contains a few remarks on the general nature of what we talk about when we speak of poetry at all; and here, I think, that if Alice's White Knight were brought in to join us, he would insist that such remarks should be called "warnings." That is not their name, of course; nor does the present occasion speak with the urgency of air-raid alarms and threats, yet something very like a "warning" is sounded every time an interpretation of poetry takes place. Unless one is actually reading the poem, hearing it, perceiving it, and is aware (for the time being) of certain hitherto unnamed emotional responses, the warning that one hears is, "What does the poem mean?" —then, a moment later—"Is the poem poetry?" From then onward we can tell you what poetry is called or has been called, but not what it is: I am inclined to think that the Wordsworth who wrote the *Ode* called it "natural piety," and that the White Knight called it "my own invention." The Gryphon and the Mock Turtle (since they were obviously concerned with matters of educational importance) undoubtedly called whatever poems they read by the name of "lessons," and most of us, like Alice, tend to respect such formidable creatures who had received the best of educations and who wept, who hid their faces in their paws at the slightest recollection of their past experiences. The pity was that lessons lessened from day to day—and that for them there had passed away a glory from the earth.

I, for one, am willing to believe that whatever the something is that is first thought of as poetry and is then given, like the White Knight's ballad, a number of different names —I believe that the kind of poetry we carry seriously in mind—soon acquires a quality that resembles an independent life, a being which springs from and yet finds a place apart from all other things in this imperfect world. As we read it, the poem exists beyond the time and the occasion that prompted its arrival; and there are moments when the poem seems to exist even beyond the gifts, the skills, the ambitions, and intentions of the person who wrote it. There are times when one might almost say that the life of a poem depends upon the varieties of misconception taking place around it; and if we are willing to agree that the play, *Hamlet*, may be read (quite as one reads the best of Shakespeare's tragedies) as a dramatic poem, surely that example should be a warning to us all. Like Hamlet's father's ghost who walks within it, the play itself still walks the earth to haunt the wariest of its interpreters. Despite the number of footnotes—or is it because of them?—that almost crowd the text of *Hamlet* off the printed page, its central being remains remarkably alive, and while it may be great joy for us to speculate on the names that it may be called, including semantics, psychology, social science or education, the independent power of life within the play is undiminished.

So it is when we approach any work conceived by human imagination: from the imperfect sources of human life, even from violent action and disorder, a selection of shapes and sounds, color and motion takes place, and we recognize that something has been done which is self-contained and active. These remarks or "warnings" are not, of course, "my own invention"; they have been spoken with far greater accuracy long ago and they may be found by those who have eyes to read them in Homer's story of the creation of Achilles' shield. The shield was an extremely cunning work of art, and its multitudinous figures resembled life so closely that the shield in its entire being seemed a mirror of the very world Achilles and his enemies had known; and we must remember that Achilles wore it to protect his body from a fatal wound. Was the shield self-knowledge? I suspect that is one of the names that it might be called.

But as I turn from Homer back to Wordsworth, and from Wordsworth to Alice, I cannot prove that Alice herself had read the whole of the famous *Ode* that asserts the promise of immortality. Others have spoken (and among them, Mr. William Empson) of Alice's perceptive wit in voicing criticism, yet I can say that her interpreter, who disguised himself as "Lewis Carroll," was not unfamiliar with the world of childhood that the Lake Poets celebrated and held before the eyes of their admirers. We know that his criticism of it was fully conscious (one has but to read the parodies he wrote while an undergraduate at Oxford), but we also know that he accepted the major premise of the *Ode*, even the vision, or rather one of those words which begin with M—the memory of the happy moment associated with the past—and if the theme of the *Ode* is closely related to the theme of growing up, certainly the theme of Alice's adventures is of the same character, and is, if anything, illuminated by a greater number of precise steps onward from childhood to maturity.

The first expression of Alice's concern about growing up reached its crisis in her interview with the Caterpillar. She was in deep trouble, and she did not, of course, wish to grow up too fast, yet she wished to be more than her three inches high. It was no wonder that the Caterpillar instructed her to recite Robert Southey's *The Old Man's Comforts*, an eminently respectable poem that had appeared in the *Youth's Magazine* for February, 1816, and since that time, it had been memorized by an entire generation of proper children. If her recitation of *Father William* did not recall the image of Wordsworth directly, the memory of Southey recalled him at his weakest, bringing to mind the unhappy *Peter Bell*, who after a wild career, saw goodness in an ass's skin, and became an honest man. From him we turn to Wordsworth's *Idiot Boy* and to *Simon Lee* and from *Simon Lee* we return to Robert Southey, the most devoted and least gifted of Wordsworth's three great friends. One remembers Dorothy Wordsworth and Coleridge readily enough, but Southey (not without cause) is as readily forgotten, and if it were not for Alice, who would care to read Southey's unconscious parody of Wordsworth's philosophic attitudes? Who would waste his time reading:

In the days of my youth, I remember'd my God!
And He hath not forgotten my age.

To these lines Alice quickly replied:

> Do you think I can listen all day to such stuff?
> Be off, or I'll kick you down stairs!

And then said timidly, "some of the words have got altered": indeed they have, and very lively words they have become. I doubt if any critic of Alice's day would have dared to go half as far as her imperfect memory carried her; and if her words "got altered," they certainly transformed the kindly, senile, sweet old Father William. Was the association also that of another William, a William Wordsworth who succeeded Southey as Poet Laureate, traveling where "other palms are won," beyond the *Ode;* was Father William the elderly poet who made petulant yet shrewd inquiries to an admirer concerning the welfare of his American investments? Perhaps Alice did not intend to go as far as that, yet her remarkably feminine (one almost says "feline") perceptions were aroused, and at the very least, her Father William knew the value of commercial enterprise and the jargon of salesmanship:

> "You are old," said the youth," as I mentioned before.
>   And have grown most uncommonly fat;
> Yet you turned a back-somersault in at the door—
>   Pray, what is the reason of that?"
>
> "In my youth," said the sage, as he shook his grey locks,
>   "I kept all my limbs very supple
> By the use of this ointment—one shilling the box—
>   Allow me to sell you a couple?"

The altered words had done their work; the recitation was not quite right. Was it fair? was it cruel? was it ethical? Alice herself was not troubled by these questions; her subconscious will had voiced its criticism, and to those who had enjoyed her version of *Father William* all questions of justice and morality were made to seem as irrelevant as the memory of conscious right and wrong within the action of a dream. But the authoritative, masculine Caterpillar who had been brought up to respect the philosophy of the Lake Poets was sure that she was wrong from beginning to end, and said so.

I shall not attempt to enlarge upon the intentions which inspired flaws in Alice's memory; we know only that she was neither deaf nor blind and that something had happened to Father William between the date of Wordsworth's *Ode* and Alice's arrival on the scene that was none too lovely to contemplate. We also know that Alice's *Father William* had been read and still continues to be read by thousands who had never heard of Southey's *The Old Man's Comforts*, and what is more important, those very readers grow restless and uncomfortable as they read the following lines from Wordsworth's *Ode:*

> The Youth, who daily farther from the east
> Must travel, still is Nature's Priest,
> And by the vision splendid
> Is on his way attended . . .

Surely, the youth in Sir John Tenniel's drawing of Father William's son (and Sir John's illustrations of Alice's adventures are not to be ignored) was a portrait of a singularly dull young man. Was he the Idiot Boy, was he Michael's son, was he Nature's Priest? Perhaps not, perhaps he was none of these, but his likeness to his brothers is scarcely short of being fatal.

Meanwhile Alice's encounter with the Caterpillar had prepared her for a more important and later crisis in growing up, and here at last, we come upon her in the dark forest attended by the White Knight whose foolish face was lit by a faint smile. The White Knight was about to sing his ballad. "It's long," said the Knight, "but it's very, *very* beautiful. Everybody that hears me sing it—either it brings the *tears* into their eyes, or else—"

"Or else what?" said Alice, for the Knight had made a sudden pause.

"Or else it doesn't, you know," replied the Knight.

The old Knight was very kindly, very gentle; he had great difficulty in staying on his horse; he was perhaps the meanest flower of knighthood; he was all too human—and there in the dark forest, and with the Knight reminding us of tears, we almost hear the strains of *Resolution and Independence*:

> Thanks to the human heart by which we live,
> Thanks to its tenderness, its joys and fears,
> To me the meanest flower that blows can give
> Thoughts that do often lie too deep for tears.

Resolution and Independence which is a far better poem than the *Ode*, and which was foreshadowed by the *Ode*, closely approached the climax of Wordsworth's poetic life; and if the poem moves in the direction of Wordsworth's maturity, a recollection of it also guides the reader in the direction of Alice with the White Knight at her side at evening in the forest. We are being prepared for the burlesque of *Resolution and Independence* in the White Knight's ballad of an aged, aged man, "the oldest man . . . that ever wore grey hairs."

> I'll tell thee everything I can:
>   There's little to relate.
> I saw an aged, aged man,
>   A-sitting on a gate.

> "Who are you, aged man?" I said.
> "And how is it you live?"
> And his answer trickled through my head,
> Like water through a sieve.

By the time the Knight completes the singing of his ballad, we are well past the *Ode*, stepping through it to the other side, quite as Alice once walked, or half-climbed, through the looking-glass. Meanwhile Lewis Carroll's criticism of Wordsworth had shifted its position of attack from indirect reference to explicit parody of a particular poem. Across that merest space from the *Ode* to contemplation of the Leech-gatherer (which is almost impossible to measure because it is so near, so far) the first of our beginnings with its images of Rousseau and the guiltless face of childhood ("A Presence which is not to be put by.") seems to tremble and dissolve as though London Bridge itself were about to fall. But Alice had already heard the crash that followed her conversation with Humpty Dumpty, and the continuous failure of well-intentioned, adult (though sometimes rude) authority no longer troubled her.

If Alice after her visit with the White Knight had begun to grow up, it was in spite of and in a totally different way than Father William and the Aged Man approved. What if she had known something of the same world that Wordsworth's *Ode* had opened to other children (and certainly to their parents and schoolmasters) of her day? The words, somehow, were not the same, and the vision of the Lake Poets had shifted its perspective—and here we must remember that Alice was a heroine and not a hero. From the White Knight she had learned of what poetry might be called, but her perceptions were becoming critical in the sense that she was soon to have other things than poetry to fill her mind. She had to say good-by to the White Knight, leap to the Eighth Square, and after a moment of dismay, be glad at last to wear a crown upon her head. Her reward was that Queen Victoria thoroughly enjoyed her adventures, for the Queen had known and witnessed the failures of masculine authority, and the weaknesses of the speculative, or as Wordsworth would have said, "the philosophic mind." Surely, her advisers and ministers had changed and fallen since she first came as a girl—scarcely a young woman—to wear the crown. There had been Grey and Melbourne, Palmerston and Peel, Derby and Lord Russell—and as for other changes, that troublesome Reform Bill was like the battle between the Lion and the Unicorn—but the Queen had outlived them all. She had outlived her Poet Laureates, Southey and Wordsworth—and the arrival of Tennyson would, no doubt, bring other changes. As for a style, a language, a fashion being laughed at, one had only to remember that in the century before Alice had been born, John Gay's *The Beggar's Opera* laughed Italian opera off the London stage.

But after this much is said of Wordsworth and Alice, why was it, granting the usual changes in poetic taste and fashion, that Wordsworth's *Ode* and its successor, *Resolution and Independence*, became so vulnerable to Alice's remarks? Unlike Achilles' shield, Wordsworth's *Ode* is by no means self-contained; it tends to fall apart, and even the most casual reader of it notices a change of temper, sensibility, and feeling that divide its opening stanzas from its last. Whatever the causes of this defect may be, surely no poet of Wordsworth's stature ever stumbled so blindly into so many traps as he. The most important of these was his undue speculation in prose on the philosophic sources of his poetry. His own definitions of poetry haunted him for fifty years of his long life, and even now, they continue to haunt academic discussions of his remains. Every school-boy can cheerfully quote and requote his eloquent phrases concerning "the spontaneous overflow of powerful feeling," yet I suspect that Wordsworth's lack of impulsiveness coupled with the mere desire to "overflow," explains many a dull passage in *The Prelude* and *The Excursion*. There can be little doubt that he accepted the rôle of being a poet with admirable seriousness, and in reading Dorothy Wordsworth's *Grasmere Journal* (1802) one can see that he approached his task with a strenuous immensity of purpose that is unequaled in English literature. In the closing stanzas of the *Ode* and through certain passages of *Resolution and Independence*, he proved his ability to make his observation, his experience, his emotions, his insights, and his thinking flow as though they traveled in a single stream, yet his longer poems contained elements of greatness rather than the completed structure of great poetry. We can sight their far distance from the self-contained design of a true poem by contrasting them with *Lycidas* and *Samson Agonistes*. Did his effort to acquire a "philosophic mind" stand in the way of his development to full maturity? The effort rewarded him with a cloak of authority which became transparent in the merest glance from Alice's candid eye.

In defense of Wordsworth, one can reply that Alice, despite her wit, despite her sharpness, lacked a perception into the tragic aspect of life that Wordsworth saw; she knew terror, but not grief; she had little concern for things outside the ranges of her immediate vision; she was a practical young female, caught, for the moment, in the mortal coils of growing up, and it is doubtful if, in her life beyond her journey through the looking-glass, one would find her meditating on the values of poetry.

Admitting that the difficulties of Wordsworth's verse

are those of memory and muchness, there are glimpses throughout it of that something, which for me, whatever name it takes, is poetry. For poetry, as I read it, is only incidentally concerned with such abstractions as "the philosophic mind," or history, or science: it need not quarrel with them, it should not quarrel with them—and on occasion, it should be aware of them to its own advantage. It has been said often enough that literary expression (being what it is) is always vitally concerned with what we call our senses—but here we must not forget our sixth sense, intelligence, for poetry must always contain something to delight the mind. Too often we credit the superior critic (and among superior critics Alice should not be forgotten) with an order of intelligence that is not to be found in poetry; this may be an unspoken hint, but it is implied. Although differences of opinion may be expressed between them, no such division exists between the gifted poet and his commentators. It is intelligence in its heightened sense, and in, I think, the best meaning of the term, that enters all poetry worthy of our attention; it implies an awareness and a sensibility reflected in the poem itself, and however subconscious, or deliberate its offices may be, it imposes those limitations that are sometimes separately regarded as poetic form; it is sensible of ethics and of the devotional spirit, and for the individual poet as well as the reader of his poetry it sometimes illuminates the darkened path toward a true knowledge of mankind.

Since this discussion threatens to expand beyond all thought of Wordsworth's *Ode* and Alice, I fear I shall return to all three of my beginnings; and it is time (if the March Hare still has his watch) for someone else to tell a story.

ON WILLIAM ERNEST HENLEY'S EDITORIAL
CAREER

WHERE is William Ernest Henley and where are the Henley evenings at the house on the road to Richmond in suburban London, a quarter-hour's walk for young men who strolled through spring twilight out from Bedford Park? *Invictus* is, of course, still remembered by those who are given to reciting verse in a loud voice, but many of the young men are gone, and if many of their names are to be recalled, they are to be found only in the files of their chief's magazines, the once famous *Observer* and the *New Review;* and today even Henley's luminaries whose fame outdistanced his, Wells of *The Time-Machine*, young Kipling of the *Barrack-Room Ballads* and *Captains Courageous*, the J. M. Barrie who wrote *Sentimental Tommy*, and Bernard Shaw who once held promise of becoming a music critic are scarcely known for what they looked like then. As for Henley himself, it is quite as though posterity had committed a special act of forgetting him and his once highly burnished reputation, his skill in marshaling the forces of literary warfare, his influence upon young men who saw him as master, chief, idol or demi-god of their generation.

It would be well, if only for a moment, to look at Henley as though he were actually restored in flesh—not the poet who wrote unrhymed verse (which seemed so "realistic" in its day) as well as ballades, triolets, and rondeaus—but as quite another kind of literary being, the careerist, the Tory critic, the hero and instructor, if you will, of young men who practiced the art of writing virulent prose. The stage directions for the scene are any afternoon or evening between 1889 and 1898; it is a room in Henley's fine house on the road to Richmond, and he is there for everyone to see. His great physique, the golden, wiry beard and hair, shoulders and upper torso thrust across a desk, or resting its full weight upon the low back of a chair, would never fail to impress his visitors with the momentousness, the urgency of all he had to say. To those who saw him in this proximity, the very atmosphere seemed charged with light, and for them it was no effort to remember the complaint of Robert Louis Stevenson's wife who had said that Henley's energy endangered Robert's health and that his friendship drove her husband to the verge of physical exhaustion.

Behind the physical presence and the impression that it left upon the imagination of Henley's young admirers, there are a few biographical facts that increased the growth of an heroic legend. Henley was born in 1849 and was the son of an unprosperous Gloucester printer and second-hand bookseller, and in addition to the fears of poverty, he suffered the privations of an incurable disease. In early adolescence, tuberculosis of the bone had maimed one foot and subsequently destroyed it. As he neared maturity, the other foot was threatened and to stave off the immediate danger of its amputation, Henley, penniless, friendless, and yet without despair made a pilgrimage from Gloucester to Edinburgh, there to make a direct appeal to the great surgeon, Lister, who became interested in his case and promptly installed him for treatment in a hospital. It was from Lister's Hospital that Henley wrote to London editors, and Sir Leslie Stephen, in particular, was stirred by the forthright character of a personality which appeared between the lines of a short letter. In February, 1875, when Sir Leslie had found occasion to visit Edinburgh, he did not forget Henley, and bringing Robert Louis Stevenson with him, called at Lister's Hospital in search of the young man whose letters had awakened such lively interest. The interview was an extraordinary success. Within an hour Henley gratified the promise that Sir Leslie had discerned in the brief letters, and at the same time, Stevenson's curiosity was transfigured into admiration for a man who so cheerfully and vigorously surmounted physical pain and economic hardship. Stevenson entered the friendship with unusual sensibility and understanding for, he too, continued to survive the threat of long illnesses. In discovering Henley he had found someone whose laughter was contagious and whose masculinity was the very complement of his own fragile graces, of his velvet-coated ease and slippered ardors.

When at last, and this was two years later, Henley arrived in London, he came as the true heir of a Danish-Anglo-Saxon family of Henleys and was, for those who saw him, the reincarnation of a Norse hero, whose ready, short-clipped phrases struck the ground as though they were as many thunder-bolts. His first venture, *London*, a satirical weekly, chose the aging Gladstone as its foil, Gladstone who was then a huge white whale swimming to its rest in warm and comfortably expanding Liberal waters. *London*'s harpoons effected little damage to the whale, but drew attention to the forceful stance and skill of a new personality in British journalism, and from an editorial office Henley emerged to receive the rewards of public recognition.

It was during the following ten years that Henley developed a remarkable aptitude for endowing the work of his contemporaries with the brilliance of his own vitality;

Austin Dobson and Alice Meynell profited greatly by his advice and championship, and with the assistance of Charles Whibley, one of his young disciples, Henley became Stevenson's literary agent, lending his energy to the support of Stevenson's early ventures in romantic fiction. When *London* perished under him (an untimely death) he sought out commissions for free-lance criticism and in a series of reviews reignited the smoldering reputation of George Meredith; he converted the *Magazine of Art* into a testing field for his esthetic convictions and in its pages he introduced the art of Rodin to the intelligence of the British public. By the time he accepted his position as editor of the *Scots Observer*, his policies for assuming a virtual dictatorship of British letters had attained full growth; and the paper was founded for the express purpose of becoming his personal vehicle.

Surely, no editor had ever received his commission on better terms than Henley's when he stepped into the office of the *Scots Observer*. Its owner was Fitz-Roy Bell, a well-to-do Scots lawyer who felt it his duty to restore Edinburgh's intellectual glory which had notably diminished since the days when Wilson and Lockhart commanded the fortunes of *Blackwood's Magazine*. Bell had read Henley's reviews and in them saw those qualities of leadership that might well equal or extend beyond the critical successes of a "Christopher North"; Bell was prepared to be generous with a man who showed every promise of filling the place that had been long left vacant by Wilson's death; the weekly journal was handsomely subsidized, and soon the wide pages of beautifully balanced type, which distinguished the *Scots Observer* from all other periodicals of its day appeared on the library tables of the British intellectuals, of the Oxford don, or undergraduate, of young men in the consular service, or the librarian—all who professed to have an interest in the latest turn of critical opinion in literature.

Self-educated and endowed with the strong will of those who climb out of poverty into the professional classes, Henley's articles of faith were those of trenchant individualism. It was characteristic of him to choose Disraeli as his political model, and in this choice lay the sources of his early strength and weakness. Through this association he earned the dislike and open distrust of the thoughtful Wilfred Scawen Blunt, and secured the protection of the nimble-witted politician, young George Wyndham. To Henley, Disraeli's drive toward the expansion of British Imperial power in the near East had all the fascination of a search for hidden treasure. Yet Henley's defense of Disraeli shows clearly enough his uneasy relationship to the object of his admiration, for the means that the statesman used ran counter to Henley's forthright disposition; and the young editor was caught in the net of semi-disillusionment which traps so many men of literary talent who follow too closely the sinuous path of political conversion.

It is, therefore, scarcely surprising to learn that a number of his contemporaries, while accepting his aid and friendship, soon adopted the habit of describing him as a literary pirate, and that Stevenson half-affectionately modeled "Long John Silver" in Henley's image. Even the least discerning of his acquaintances saw in his worship of physical strength a compensatory impulse toward balancing his own physical disabilities—and that impulse soon showed its nakedness as it translated itself into editorial tyranny. From the very start of Henley's career on the *Observer*, he had used the periodical as a training school for his young men, young men who displayed either personal loyalty to himself or unusual promise of pursuing a literary apprenticeship as stern as his own had been and as prolific. Once they had proved their usefulness, the young men were then trained to submit to Henley's explicit orders: "Never again use that detestable word, 'stylist,' if you would be an officier of mine" he wrote to Vernon Blackburn, and the instruction was like an order of the day.

Henley's successful leadership, however, built castles of sand against an eventual and seemingly inevitable storm. As Blunt observed, he was "a bitter talker, but a sayer of good things," and as he grew older, the bitterness increased; his quarrels became more frequent, and were, at times, patently unnecessary. He had been among the first to champion and to publish the poetry of W. B. Yeats, and he could not refrain from the urge of rewriting the poems that had been submitted to him. I doubt if the exercise of this prerogative deeply stirred the currents of Yeats's enmity, but in after years, when Yeats wrote of the time that he also frequented the Henley evenings, one finds his enthusiasm for Henley's gifts considerably cooled. He remarked that he had been comforted by the knowledge that Henley also rewrote Kipling's verse, but it is significant that Yeats recalls on the very same page of his *Autobiography* an encounter with a former member of Henley's once formidable reviewing staff:

I met him in Paris, very sad and, I think, very poor. "Nobody will employ me now," he said. "Your master is gone," I answered, "and you are like the spear in an old Irish story that had to be kept dipped in poppy-juice that it might not go about killing people on its own account."

Henley's falling out with Bernard Shaw was a matter of far more serious concern; Henley was among the first to recognize the potential qualities of Shaw's work; and with a commanding, impatient, enthusiastic gesture of approval, Henley insisted that Shaw write his essays in musical criticism for the *Observer*. Shaw immediately agreed to contribute a series of commentaries on current events in music and all went well until the question of Richard Wagner's latest work arose. In London, appreciation of Wagner's symphonic operas had been nursed to shrill and feverish heights by members of the Pre-Raphaelite Brotherhood, all of whom were marked targets for Henley's bitterest scorn. In a weekly article commissioned by the *Observer* Shaw spoke well of Wagner and Henley accepted it; but when the piece appeared in print Shaw found that his praise of Wagner had been changed to censure by Henley's unmistakable turn of phrasing. Shaw cut short his friendship with the *Observer's* editor, and the break was final. From that time onward he chose to overlook Henley's merits and to dismiss him (not without kindly patronage) as unimportant, as a minor poet to whom matter meant little and manner everything.

Throughout Henley's long-extended quarrel with the Pre-Raphaelite Brotherhood, he held the position of a man whose tastes were austere and positive, but whose judgment in phrasing them reduced a sound and intelligent thesis to the levels of petty controversy. One can understand and readily underscore his dislike of the rhetoric which so lavishly embellished Rossetti's sonnets in *The House of Life:* and there can be small doubt that Henley would have welcomed Gerard Manley Hopkins' remarks upon the infirmities of Swinburne's diction, particularly in the observation that had been made to Canon Dixon as early as the winter of 1881:

Swinburne is a strange phenomenon: His poetry seems a powerful effort at establishing a new standard of poetical diction, of the rhetoric of poetry; but to waive every other objection it is essentially archaic, biblical a good deal, and so on: now that is a thing that can never last. . . .

In turn one can approve of Henley's stricture as he wrote: "An artist is he who knows how to select and to inspire the results of his selection," a remark which anticipates by a quarter-century Ezra Pound's advice to his followers in *A Retrospect* republished in 1918: "We shall have fewer painted adjectives impending the shock . . . As for myself, I want it so, austere, direct, free from emotional slither . . . In the art of Daniel and Cavalcanti, I have seen that precision which I miss in the Victorians—that explicit rendering, be it of external nature, or of emotion."

But it must be admitted that Henley seemed to be a shade too openly preoccupied with the popular successes through which the Pre-Raphaelite Brotherhood exerted its influence. An occasion presented itself for him to attack Rossetti's privately printed magazine, the *Germ,* and with a recklessness that brought him little honor, he remarked:

Dante Rossetti imagined the *Germ,* made the *Germ* possible, floated the *Germ,* and in the long run died of the *Germ.* The engineer "hoist with his own petard" was never better exampled than in Dante Rossetti and the magazine which excused his lapses and made him an amateur for the term of his natural life.

To this day one is tempted to believe that the humorless invectives Henley employed to crush his adversaries restored them to admiration among sensitive and uncritical readers, and it is not at all improbable that the violence of his abuse momentarily elevated the Rossettis, Dante Gabriel and his industrious brother, William, to the eminence of literary martyrdom. Like the unfortunate Robert Buchanan, whose essay, *The Fleshly School of Poetry,* had achieved sufficient notoriety to condemn the critical reputation of its author, Henley seemed to have "fought because he could not think."

Meanwhile many doubts concerning the seriousness of Pre-Raphaelite scholarship had been set in motion by John Churton Collins, one of Henley's friends, whose long report on the state of learning at Oxford and Cambridge universities contained a withering list of errors that had caught his eye in Sir Edmund Gosse's studies in English literature which had been published under the imposing title, *From Shakespeare to Pope*. In speaking of Churton Collins in this particular place I hope I may be pardoned for seeming to digress from the downward stream of Henley's career in journalism. The two men had like temperamental affinities, and if Henley's tyrannies had made it far too easy for a succeeding generation to forget his energy and courage, the memory of Collins's name and reputation have been lost in an obscurity so deep that they awaken greater curiosity than a sober interest in the values he represented. In memoirs written by minor figures of late Victorian celebrity Collins is remembered chiefly as the man who once insulted "poor Gosse" by listing the many errors he had made—and the single appreciation of Collins's weight in modern criticism finds its voice in Mr. T. S. Eliot's essay on Cyril Tourneur.

Collins entered the field of critical scholarship by a road no less difficult than Henley's journey from Lister's Hospital to London. As an undergraduate at Balliol, Collins had shown extraordinary promise, but he left Oxford without taking his degree and came down to London to face poverty and the dreary routine of teaching classical literature at Scoones's Training School for Indian and Civil Service. An appointment to lecture in the University Extension system came to him as an act of deliverance from Scoones, yet nine-tenths of his waking hours were spent on lecture platforms, for he had joined a small army of bright young men who were sent with lecture notes in one hand and a watch in the other to distribute the mysteries of learning, classical or otherwise, to large middle-class audiences throughout London and its neighboring boroughs. The position, if it could be called such, was scarcely one that enhanced his authority in the writing of critical articles; anything he wrote was likely to be viewed (which it was) as taking root from an extra-mural source, and when his critical report on the universities appeared in the pages of the *Quarterly Review* for December, 1886, Collins was a man of thirty-eight, and the many years of talk in lecture halls, of hasty note-taking, of being hard-pressed for time had left their ugly scars upon his prose.

It was all too easy to dismiss Collins's passion for reform in the universities as seeming heretical in the sense Gosse wished his strictures to be read, for Collins vehemently distrusted the value of teaching literature in the manner of the German philologists, a method which then dominated professional scholarship at Oxford and Cambridge; and at the other extreme, Collins with equal vehemence also distrusted the loose, drawling, drawing-room manner of Gosse's entry into literary criticism. In the light of Collins's excellent studies in the literature of the sixteenth and seventeenth centuries, including his revaluation of John Dryden which was the first and is still the most impressive study of its kind in modern criticism, there is little doubt that the best of his work has improved with the passage of time. One finds it salutary to quote or underline a passage from his essay on the study of classical literature in the universities:

Classical literature can never become extinct, but it can lose its vogue, it can become the almost exclusive possession of mere scholars, it can cease to be influential . . . Philology cannot save it. It must be linked with life to live, with the incarnation of that of which it too is the incarnation, to prevail. Associate it as poetry with poetry, as oratory with oratory, as criticism with criticism and it will be vital and mighty.

Collins's early friendship with Swinburne which had been broken by the intervention of Sir Edmund Gosse, bore the fruits of his studies in dramatic poetry, and his was perhaps the first of many rediscoveries of John Donne which continued from his day into the first quarter of the twentieth century.

Among the many reasons why Collins's ventures into criticism failed to attract the readers of its day and is left for us to rediscover in its oblivion, is that Collins, in his position as a radical-Conservative, stood aside from the larger currents of popular feeling which warmed and nourished Gladstone's retreat in Liberal waters; to attack Gosse's scholarship was to attack by implication the rise of Liberal opinion in Great Britain, and Collins's brusque dismissal of William Rossetti's scholarship also implied to the casual reader a counter-thrust at the entire Pre-Raphaelite Brotherhood, including the robust and vigorously combative William Morris who had served so notoriously as a figurehead in the ranks of Socialism.

Another important cause of Churton Collins's failure to move easily among his contemporaries, and here his fate with Henley's carried its burden to posterity, was his unguarded and probably unconscious love of controversy for its own sake, an emotion which in its awkward sincerity, quite as William Hazlett's urgency to confess his domestic misfortunes, still embarrasses the reader. The lack of an early success in his career clouded the last few years of Collins's life, for even his appointment to a chair at the University of Birmingham had come too late, and he had felt, not without reason, that his literary remains would be forgotten.

Nor were the closing years of Henley's life less unfortunate in their Cassandra-like decline into disfavor; as his sense of personal loss increased with the death of a young daughter, his quarrels became even more frequent and ill-advised, yet however cynical he may have become, he was not as Stevenson implied (a hint that touched off a series of erratic estrangements between the two men) a man bent upon filling his purse at the cost of literature. Even the later *Observer*, which had changed its prefix from *Scots* to *National* and the more impressive *New Review* which followed it, refused to compromise its values by publishing work that could be described as merely cheap or popular. Whatever excesses in tactlessness or anger he may have indulged in at the expense of critical sanity and justice, Henley, the editor, remained the watchful, energetic guardian of what was then a new and unknown generation in English letters—and in that office he was incorruptible, if not serene.

Perhaps it was a self-destructive impulse, and surely it was one nurtured in bitterness, that led Henley to write his essay on Robert Louis Stevenson for the pages of *Pall Mall's Magazine*. After a moment of hesitation, Henley agreed to review Balfour's official biography of *R. L. S.* for *Pall Mall's* book section, but as he began to write, he soon discovered that Stevenson's death had not resolved the emotional difficulties which had unsettled the latter years of their relationship; his patience broke, and his essay rambled into an unsavory reminiscence of old quarrels. In reply to Henley's ill-timed recklessness and critical irrelevancies, the British public was willing to accept Oscar Wilde's remark that so nearly touched the source of Henley's weakness: "He has always thought too much about himself which is wise; and written too much about others that is foolish."

Henley's essay on Stevenson was the last of his controversial appearances, and in the year of his death, two years later, in 1903, he felt that he had survived all his disciples, and certainly, he had lived beyond his short span of great literary fame. One rereads his famous *Invictus* as one might read an ironic epitaph on a hard-won and ill-poised integrity—and last of all, one hears the failing echo of a spent career. He was not the master of his fate, for the ambitions of the world had been too much with him, its glories were of the transitory powers emanating from an editor's desk and chair; they were of the visions that floated across proof-sheets waiting correction under the lamp, and their illusion of an enduring life had vanished almost as soon as Henley's body had found its rest within the grave.

ON GEORGE MOORE AND REGIONALISM
IN REALISTIC FICTION

IN America, the literary fashions of the 1880's and the 1890's which had been imported from continental Europe and its islands, enjoyed an irresponsible and certainly indecorous old age until the years immediately following the first World War. This has been particularly true of our relations to British literature of Yellow Book origins and to the tradition of Flaubert, and in this respect we have been slower than the Germans. Someone—I believe it was D. H. Lawrence—said that Thomas Mann was "the last sick sufferer from the complaint of Flaubert," but Flaubert was not generally appreciated as a serious novelist in the United States until 1919! By that time, we had belatedly discovered George Moore—and not the George Moore who has always and still deserves a measure of our attention, but he who had written *Confession of a Young Man*, the George Moore who had so flagrantly enjoyed the liberties he had taken in writing and re-editing his dead life. We embraced his foolishness, his indiscretions; and we shared, vicariously, of course, his love of shocking those who were supposedly a shade more innocent than he. We enjoyed half-seriously his belated impersonations of Huysmans, Pater, Wilde, and Gautier—but admiration of this kind grew chilly beyond the third decade of the present century, and at the moment of his death in 1933, his literary remains had begun to fall, soundlessly and with scant honors, into the semi-obscurity in which they rest today.

If one makes allowances for the slight embarrassments which attend a revival of recently outmoded literary figures, a rereading of George Moore's early novels is by no means difficult. The only difficulty that arises is the possible mistake of taking their author too seriously, but one does not stop reading; something is there that outlives the moment of its creation. One decides to follow the heroine of *A Mummer's Wife* to her last fifth of gin in a London slum, one pauses to take another look (and not without amusement) at Lewis Seymour in *A Modern Lover* boldly posed naked (he was to represent a dancing faun) in Mrs. Bentham's drawing room. One then recalls how swiftly and how skillfully Moore introduced the latest fashions in French naturalism to the subscribers of London's circulating libraries. This was in the early 1880's and at a moment when the very thought of translating Zola into English for the enlightenment of the British public seemed both highly experimental and morally dangerous. Perhaps a reason why the libraries (after a brief dispute) decided to accept Moore was that it must have been as difficult to take Moore seriously then as it is today. Moore earnestly defended his lack of humor, but the spirit which his early books convey has the charm, the occasional turn of brilliant observation, the eagerness, the sensitivity of the obviously immature, yet gifted writer.

One agrees that the circulating libraries took small risk in allowing *A Modern Lover* and *A Mummer's Wife* to pass from hand to hand among young British matrons or their housemaids. The books may well have been shocking, but the incidents that were artfully contrived to shock us are so innocently, so boyishly confided and so lightly placed and stressed; they had the air of being "entertainments," rather than the weighted arguments that would blast the family hearth or endanger the Stock Exchange. Despite the skill with which Moore handled the formulae of naturalism, despite his exact descriptions of airless and shabby rooms or fog-darkened streets, his scenes of Paris and of London lack emotional reality, quite as they lack the realities of verbal warmth and density and color. It was not until his third novel was written, *A Drama in Muslin*, in 1886, that one could possibly discern a third-dimensional quality at work; there, the scene is well within the English pale of Ireland, and is circumscribed by journeys to and from Dublin's Viceregal court, the parlors of the Shelbourne Hotel, and Anglo-Irish estates and country houses.

Since I believe that George Moore was indisputably an Irish writer rather than an Irishman who had acquired British poise, the occasion arises for a brief commentary on the regional aspects of naturalism in fiction. One should not be surprised to find Moore at his best on Irish soil, for the premise of his consciously acquired art (the realistic novel in its latest form) almost demanded that he should have been, but before I enlarge upon the Anglo-Irish character of Moore's work, what seems both a truism and a paradox in the esthetics of realism should be given a hearing.

The realistic novel, as we have known it, is of protean shapes; it is of many tongues and of many varieties, depths, and colors. It is easy to agree that Fielding, Gogol, Tolstoy, Balzac, Flaubert, Dickens, Nexö, Dreiser, and the Thomas Mann who wrote his *Buddenbrooks* were realistic novelists. The mask that realism wears is international and yet the hidden limitations of the realistic novel are regional. The best and most far-reaching examples of its art depend upon an intimate awareness to a particular environment; the particulars of human behavior present their immediate problems to the author and reader alike, for both must feel the external truth of what is being said and done. It has taken a second World War with its news of a north-eastern front extending into the far reaches of the Russian plains to endow Tolstoy's *War and Peace* with a renewed vitality for the American reader. And those readers who cannot carry in the mind's eye the omnipresent, yellow-gray density of fog in nineteenth century London would also fail to grasp the full meaning of the theme and its variations in Dickens's masterpiece, *Bleak House*. As one follows the mutations of realism and its heirs in the novels of Zola in France, of George Moore in Ireland, of Dreiser, Sherwood Anderson, and James T. Farrell in the American Middle-West, the writer's awareness of a particular time and place seems to increase; he tends to grow more and more dependent upon the realities of an environment and a region that he knows well, and with this knowledge, he conveys the strength of his convictions to his reader. To the foreign reader he demands an effort in the direction of an accurate translation—and lacking that effort, the best of his serious writing is likely to become transformed into a novel of exotic charm, as though it were a trip to a strange place, in which the wilds of urban Chicago, New York, or Paris, may assume (to the reader's eye) the same attraction that is felt in reading an account of a journey to the source of an unknown river in Brazil. In this sense, many a realistic novel offers the blandishments of an "escape" for the bored or harried reader; and, often enough, the very rich have enjoyed the exotic charms of a novel relating the misfortunes of the very poor.

George Moore's eager and enthusiastic practice of the arts of realism, even today, has an air of seeming fresh and adventurous. He did not seem to move at a measured pace, but to leap and to dive, swimming through gaps in his own inventions by hasty adaptations of scenes and episodes from the novels of Flaubert and Zola; the water was cold, but he churned its surface until it sparkled. If the successes of *A Modern Lover* and *A Mummer's Wife* did not bring him fame, they suddenly illuminated the curious aura of notoriety that was always to be associated with the mention of his name; and the phenomenon deceived a number of his critics, Virginia Woolf among them, into thinking that his gifts were exclusively those which enabled him to write his fictional autobiographies; and there is little to show that he himself was not equally deceived, for George Moore, as his *Confessions* and his *Memoirs of My Dead Life* so plainly testify, was unable to make a clear distinction between notoriety and fame. A transitory burst of candor meant as much to him as an arduous search for truth, and he mistook the surprise he caused by the first for the more difficult achievements of the latter. It was candor that betrayed Moore's lack of true worldliness; and his confidences, whispered aloud for all the world to hear ("Moore never kissed but told"), left him naked to the rebukes of his more seriously minded contemporaries. Bernard Shaw's stage directions and prefaces to his plays, even when they had the air of taking the reader or spectator into personal confidence, never failed of their objective in social criticism; in Moore's voice, the personal aside was less clearly directed and controlled, and however often it ridiculed the canons of Victorian respectability, it frequently lapsed into what seemed to be the utterance of a deliberately phrased *faux pas*.

But between the writing of his first two novels and his *Confessions of a Young Man*, Moore wrote the earliest of three books that merit our attention, *A Drama in Muslin*, and, as if to strengthen and support my argument that Moore's work was at its happiest at home, the book was actually written in Ireland. The training he had received in

Paris (for the city of Paris had been his university and Manet, Turgenev, and Zola may be regarded as his instructors) began to bear the fruits of his industry. Within ten years he had been transformed from an Anglo-Irish dilettante, born to an estate that yielded several hundreds of pounds per annum, into an industrious novelist and man of letters—and in Dublin he possessed the advantage gained by a lack of celebrity at home. If in a later generation, Joyce saw the Dublin of his *Ulysses* with a steadier and more deeply penetrating eye than Moore, we should remember that Moore was there before him, viewing the city with a gaze of youthful detachment and a true concern for the arts of prose. In *A Drama in Muslin*, Moore's acknowledged spokesman is a Mr. John Harding, a novelist, who drifts, almost unseen, through Dublin streets and through the reception rooms of the Shelbourne Hotel; he is an object of admiration for Moore's plain-featured, shy, and humorless little heroine, Alice Barton, but the admiration does not grow into love, for Mr. Harding remains her self-appointed guardian and educator.

In rereading *A Drama in Muslin* one half-envies those who discovered Moore as a promising young novelist in the 1880's; as in *A Modern Lover* and *A Mummer's Wife* his lack of maturity was again turned to his advantage; and even today, one feels that his sensibilities heralded the awakening of a new spirit in modern fiction. The marriage market of an Anglo-Irish gentry at Dublin's viceregal court was the object of Moore's concern and ironic observation; the court is gone, and the immediate occasion for Moore's protest against the fate of innocent and badly educated young men and women, paired off and sold at the marriage market by ambitious mothers and bankrupt fathers has long since passed. But to view sex clearly as a marketable social commodity was a position taken up by Bernard Shaw a few years later in *Mrs. Warren's Profession*, and the close juxtapositions of extreme wealth and extreme poverty which created so much dramatic and intellectual excitement in Shaw's early plays have their premiere in *A Drama in Muslin*. If Turgenev had read and admired Maria Edgeworth and learned from her a measure of the skill required in writing a realistic novel of social irony, Moore had been no less assiduous in taking hints from Turgenev's discoveries in reading *Castle Rackrent* and *The Absentee*. An inspired cycle of literary apprenticeships had come to a full round and returned to its source within the English pale in Ireland. But Moore's sensibilities were also tuned to receive all the protests of a youthful generation that had been caught in the net of elderly ambitions, mistakes, and Victorian hypocrisies.

It is not just to say that Moore lacked art in the writing of *A Drama in Muslin;* yet its atmosphere of something we call an artless charm pervades throughout the narrative; we enjoy it in much the same spirit that we find pleasure in witnessing an earnest and enthusiastic rehearsal of a play in a small town six weeks before its arrival ten doors west of Broadway; the director is inspired and is willing to risk a few experiments in technique that an older and perhaps wiser man would consciously avoid and the actors are doing better (if one makes allowances for awkward pauses and incompleted gestures) than they know. The episodic and simultaneous shift of scene between a landowner bargaining with rebellious tenants, and his wife bargaining for the sale of his pretty daughter is a venture into the experimental techniques of realistic fiction that has been continued from the day *A Drama in Muslin* first appeared to the writing of John Dos Passos' *42nd Parallel*. The characters of Mrs. Barton, the scheming mother, who learns too late the feminine unwisdom of turning each rival mother with a girl for sale into an enemy, the stupid beauty, her daughter Olive, her husband, the landlord who fancies himself a painter of unrecognized talents, the young Lord Kilcarney, the "catch" of the Dublin season, who is besieged alike by rapacious mothers and starving tenants, are memorably and sensitively drawn. Moore's improvisions were those of an exceptionally bright student of realistic fiction who had suddenly usurped the master's place and had become for one brief hour the teacher, and if not the philosopher, the guide. In sensibility he had advanced beyond all other younger novelists of his day; only the mature Henry James with his virtually unread and certainly unappreciated *Princess Casamassima* overshadowed him, and in the position he had won, he attained a freedom of eloquence and a quickness of perception which in many of his later novels and in their numerous revisions were either stilled or blotted from the page.

In *A Drama in Muslin* he had found almost too much to say on too many varied subjects, but all were related to his discontent of living in Ireland.

The Dublin streets [he wrote] stare the vacant and helpless stare of a beggar selling matches on a doorstep. . . . On either side of you, there is bawling ignorance or plaintive decay. . . . We are in a land of echoes and shadows. . . . Is there a girl or young man in Dublin who has read a play of Shakespeare, a novel of Balzac, a poem of Shelley? Is there one who could say for certain that Leonardo da Vinci was neither a comic-singer nor patriot?—No. Like children, the young and old, run hither and thither, seeking in Liddell oblivion of the Land League. Catholic in name, they curse the Pope for not helping them in their affliction; moralists by tradition, they accept at their parties women who parade their lovers to the town from the top of a tramcar. In Dublin there is baptism in tea and communion in a cutlet.

The discontent that Moore displayed was salutary and one feels that he expressed it with deeper penetration into the lives of a people than the kind of social criticism he had to offer later in the pages of *Esther Waters* and *Evelyn Innes*. One does not easily forget the scene in which the weak and bewildered young Lord Kilcarney wanders alone on the stone embankments of the Liffey in the small, dark hours of the morning, pursued by promises of ambitious mothers with marriageable daughters and harried by threats of economic ruin promised with equal vehemence by Parnell and the Land League.

Looking backward and in that glance reviewing the social dramas of Bernard Shaw, the pamphlets and speeches of the Fabian Society, the domestic novels of Arnold Bennett, and the H. G. Wells of *Mr. Polly* and *Tono-Bungay*, the flashes of youthful insight which illuminate the narrative of *A Drama in Muslin* seem at this distance to have acquired the prophetic intonations of a Delphic oracle. As the novel closes, one reads the following description of Ashbourne Crescent in London:

To some this air of dull well-to-do-ness may seem as intolerable, as obscene in its way as the look of melancholy silliness which the Dubliners and their dirty city wear so unintermittently. One is the inevitable decay which must precede an outburst of national energy; the other is the smug optimism, that fund of materialism, on which a nation lives, and which in truth represents the bulwarks wherewith civilisation defends itself against those sempiternal storms which, like atmospheric convulsions, by destroying, renew the tired life of man. And that Ashbourne Crescent, with its bright brass knockers, its white-capped maidservant, and spotless oilcloths, will in the dim future pass away before some great tide of revolution that is now gathering strength far away, deep down and out of sight in the heart of the nation, is probable enough; but it is certainly now, in all its cheapness and vulgarity, more than anything else representative, though the length and breadth of the land be searched, of the genius of Empire that has been glorious through the long tale that nine hundred years have to tell. . . .

It is in Ashbourne Crescent that Moore's solemn and candid heroine became a successful lady novelist and it was there, happily wedded to a physician, that she came to rest; the comedy was over, and Moore's little study in social irony had a satisfactory and plausible conclusion.

Moore's return to Ireland at the end of the century (as everyone who has read his *Hail and Farewell* remembers) had been inspired by W. B. Yeats's enthusiasm and his urgent propaganda for a Celtic Renaissance in literature. By this time Moore's celebrity in London was well established, and the temperamental differences which always existed and were never resolved between the two men, had been shrewdly put aside by Yeats with the purpose of using Moore's gifts and notoriety to support a worthy cause. I happen to believe that Yeats's invitation came to Moore at a critical moment in his career, that it prolonged his creative life by another decade, and we, as readers of Moore's half-forgotten novels, are enriched by a rediscovery of *The Lake* and *The Untilled Field*. Among Moore's weaknesses as a mature writer (and despite his industry) was his infinite capacity for being bored; the boredom was all the more insidious because Moore lacked sufficient self-knowledge to realize its effect upon his work. The curse of dullness which is so brilliantly absent from his early novels and his scenes of life in Ireland, begins its round in the pages of *Esther Waters* and is resumed after the completion of *Hail and Farewell* to continue till the end of his life which closed so inauspiciously with *Aphrodite in Aulis* and *The Pastoral Loves of Daphnis and Chloe* and *Peronnik the Fool*. When Yeats's invitation came, Moore had the need to be prodded back to the centers of his discontent, to be made aware of them in such fashion that his active sensibilities could be reawakened. I am not prepared to say that Yeats fully perceived the importance of his urgent invitation to George Moore; I suspect not, I suspect that he was too deeply concerned with his own relationship to the Celtic Renaissance to realize that he had granted Moore more than a passing favor. I am inclined to believe that their subsequent quarrels had at their source an esthetic (and therefore far less flagrantly personal) cause of disagreement than certain passages in *Hail and Farewell* and Yeats's *Dramatis Personae* would seem to indicate. Moore was an excellently well-trained and sensitive critic of modern painting while Yeats was a notably inept one; Moore was a naïvely schooled and indifferent critic of verse which his *Anthology of Pure Poetry* proved to all the world, while Yeats in his own voice as a poet commanded an authority that was and still remains superior to almost everything that Moore might have to say concerning poetry. It is impossible to speak of Yeats's work without acknowledging the far reach inward to the realities of subjective being while the delights of reading Moore's prose are those which are gained by reading the observations of a man who has been inspired by the presence of an active world around him.

But whatever the causes of Moore's reawakening of energy may have been, the stories which Moore included in *The Untilled Field* remain as fresh today as in the hour that he wrote them to be translated into Irish in 1900. The spirit in which he composed them was cheerfully stressed in his preface to the Carra Edition of *The Untilled Field* in 1923:

. . . I wrote "The Wedding Gown," "Alms-Giving," "The Clerk's Quest," and "So On He Fares," in English rather than in Anglo-Irish, for of what help would that pretty idiom, in which we catch the last accents of the original language, be to Tiagh Donoghue, my translator? . . . but these first stories begot a desire to paint the portrait of my country, and this could only be done in a Catholic atmosphere. . . . The Exile rose up in my mind quickly, and before putting the finishing hand to it I began "Home Sickness." The village of Duncannon in the story set me thinking of the villages around Dublin, and I wrote "Some Parishioners," "Patchwork," "The Wedding Feast," and "The Window." The somewhat harsh rule of Father Maguire set me thinking of a gentler type of priest, and the pathetic figure of Father MacTurnan tempted me. I wrote "A Letter to Rome" and "A Play-House in the Waste"; and as fast as these stories were written they were translated into Irish. . . .

With the aid of a literal translation (done by T. W. Rolleston) of a few of the stories back into their original English, Moore edited *The Untilled Field* for British and American publication; Gaelic imagery had strengthened the original text, and the stories were, as he wrote, "much improved by their bath in Irish. 'She had a face such as one sees in a fox' . . . how much better than 'She had a fox-like face.' "

The little stories, sketches, and a novelette, *The Wild Goose* which are listed in the contents of *The Untilled Field* were never widely read, and Moore himself confessed that he had half-forgotten their existence because he was so soon engaged in writing a sequel to them in *The Lake*. Perhaps the lack of appreciation they received injured Moore's vanity, but it is more likely, that coming as they did from a semi-conscious source of inspiration, Moore underrated their importance, and presented them with a display of too much modesty. Something of their true quality is suggested in the speech of the anonymous spectator who tells the story of the blind man in *Alms-Giving:*

The new leaves were beginning in the high branches. I was sitting where sparrows were building their nests, and very soon I seemed to see further into life than I had ever seen before. "We're here," I said, "for the purpose of learning what life is, and the blind beggar has taught me a great deal, something that I could not have learnt out of a book, a deeper truth than any book contains. . . ."

In this spirit Moore created his Father Maguire, the stupidly domineering priest, and Father MacTurnan, the innocent and heroically humane father of his parish and with them there is the remarkable Biddy M'Hale who caused Father Maguire so much trouble by donating the money for a window in his new church and following her, there is the story of *The Wild Goose,* the repatriated Anglo-Irish newspaperman, whose career as a politician in Ireland has its broad analogy to the career of Parnell, and among the best of the shorter pieces is *The Wedding Gown* in which Moore's sensibility reminds one of the qualities that are discovered in rereading the tales of Hans Christian Andersen. In his introduction to the Carra Edition of *The Untilled Field,* it was characteristic of the later Moore to claim that his Irish stories served as a precedent for John Synge's *The Playboy of the Western World,* but whether they did or not (and I suspect that they did not) the quality of their prose and the sensitivity of their observations foreshadowed the writing of Joyce's *Dubliners. The Untilled Field* contains no story as well controlled or as delicately contrived as Joyce's little masterpiece, *The Dead,* but the reaches of *The Untilled Field* closely approximate the intentions and accomplishments of Joyce's stories, and with the exceptions of Joyce's *The Dead* and *A Little Cloud*, Moore's stories are markedly superior.

To us who read Moore at a trans-Atlantic distance and at a time when his once-spectacular introduction of literary modes and attitudes seem outworn, an interesting and seemingly far-fetched analogy—a parallel, if you will—between George Moore and Sherwood Anderson comes to mind. For a moment, the parallel seems curious rather than exact, but the more I think of it, the closer the work of the two writers falls together, and the analogy which seemed to span too great a distance between them reveals something that results in a just understanding and estimate of their contributions, each separately, to a national literature.

Like Moore, Anderson indulged himself in a wealth of semi-autobiographical reminiscence and extolled the merits of candor above those of truth, and like Moore's autobiographies, Anderson's memoirs and storyteller's stories seem less like actual confessions than works of fiction that had been released from the disciplines employed by writing a short story or a novel. To a notable degree both men as writers lost themselves among the high arches and corridors of the palace of art. In later life, Moore returned to his early and ill-advised worship of Walter Pater, and his habits of industry kept him chained to the task of writing the books which now seemed fated for oblivion. With equal misfortune, Anderson's love of the perfect phrase, the prose sentence, and paragraph that remain an eternal delight to the eye and ear seems to have sterilized the gifts that promised so brilliant a future in the two volumes of his short stories, *Winesburg, Ohio* and *The Triumph of the Egg.* If Moore's source of inspiration lay within the English pale surrounding Dublin, certainly the sources of the sensibilities that Anderson so memorably expressed may be found within an equally small circumference of Midwestern small towns, railway junctions, and farm lands; and the resemblance between the work of the two men increases as one remembers the debt that a younger generation of writers owed to them. To the same degree that *A Drama in Muslin*, *The Untilled Field*, and *The Lake* anticipated the discernments of a new literary generation in Anglo-Irish—and indeed, British—literature, Anderson's early short stories preceded the now familiar complex of youthful sensibility and a concern for artful presentation, of naturalism and of individual candor that is so strongly marked in the early writings of Hemingway, Faulkner, and Dos Passos. Both elder writers possessed the impulse "to see further into life," something that could not be learned out of a book and was "a deeper truth than any book contains." This impulse is, of course, by no means an uncommon impulse in any generation, but Moore's and Anderson's discovery and expression of it, set an example for the young writers who came after them.

It would be easy to regard Moore's long career in writing prose a failure, and it is certainly easy for me to repeat that the expectations he awakened were never quite fulfilled, that the very terms of his art (those of the naturalistic novel) left him discontented, that he never perceived fully the richness and value of his Irish origins even as they were displayed in his own writing. The almost fatal lack of knowing fully his true identity with Ireland cut him off from those sources of feeling which might have resulted in work of lesser scope than he enjoyed, and would have been of more mature and lasting satisfaction. Easy as it may be to enlarge his failures and dimmed as Moore's reputation seems today, the scales of a final judgment still tip in his favor. I have repeatedly spoken of his sensibility, and I have done so because everything he wrote reflects the writer whose art is guided by feeling rather than the deeper inward reaches of emotion. Few writers survive the trials of writing their autobiographies—a last farewell that should be taken late in life—and Moore, after his confessions and memoirs of a dead life, retained enough energy to write his third and best, *Hail and Farewell*, which overshadowed the merits of his more pretentious novels. The sensibility of which I speak had its moments of a significant hold on the imagination and its presence distinguishes Moore from all other writers of prose in English who suffered the transition which carried them from the nineteenth century into the twentieth. One thinks of Moore's survival in much the same terms as Father Oliver's swim to safety in the closing pages of *The Lake:*

A long mile of water lay between him and Joycetown, but there was a courage he had never felt before in his heart, and a strength he had never felt before in his limbs. Once he stood up in the water, sorry that the crossing was not longer. "Perhaps I shall have had enough of it before I get there"; and he turned on his side and swam half a mile before changing his stroke. He changed it and got on his back because he was beginning to feel cold and tired, and soon after he began to think that it would be about as much as he could do to reach the shore. A little later he was swimming frog-fashion, but the change did not seem to rest him, and seeing the shore still a long way off he began to think that perhaps after all he would find his end in the lake. His mind set on it, however, that the lake should be foiled, he struggled on, and when the water shallowed he felt he had come to the end of his strength.

"Another hundred yards would have done for me," he said, and he was so cold that he could not think, and sought his clothes vaguely, sitting down to rest from time to time among the rocks.

"How cold are thy baths, Apollo" is the phrase that returns to mind whenever one thinks of Moore; and in a literature of Anglo-Irish origins, we think of him as one who shook himself free, if only for a brief hour, of the chilling waters of Apollo, and who is now on the fortunate shores of an immortality.

ON WILLIAM BUTLER YEATS AND THE
MASK OF JONATHAN SWIFT

All my life I have been haunted with the idea that the poet should know all classes of men as one of themselves. Some day setting out to find knowledge, like some pilgrim to The Holy Land he will become the most romantic characters. He will play with all masks.

> —*Estrangement*, extracts from
> a Diary kept in 1909.

> Put off that mask of burning gold
> With emerald eyes
> O no my dear, you make so bold
> To find if hearts be wild and wise
> And yet not cold.

> —"The Mask," from *The Green
> Helmet and Other Poems*. 1910

> I declare this tower is my symbol: I declare
> This winding, gyring, spiring treadmill of a stair is my
>   ancestral stair:
> That Goldsmith and the Dean, Berkeley and Burke have
>   travelled there:
> Swift beating on his breast in sibylline frenzy blind
> Because the heart in his blood-sodden breast has dragged
>   him down into mankind.

> —*The Winding Stair*. 1929

136

In rereading the poetry of William Butler Yeats's last decade, one need not and, indeed, one should not believe everything one sees and hears. The last and fourth period of Yeats's creative life was in some respects his most fruitful period; surely it brought to him his years of widest fame and seemed to uncover new sources of his matured imagination—and yet, even as we recognize and pay tribute to his gifts as a lyric poet, we should not overlook his talent as an actor, an actor who richly cultivated his poetic attitudes, who wore many masks and spoke in many voices, and whose work at proper intervals contained, as he himself would have been pleased to say, "the fascination of the difficult."

Remembering his autobiographies, from the earliest *Reveries over Childhood and Youth* to the last of his published reminiscences, *Dramatis Personae*, and not forgetting George Moore's *Hail and Farewell*, one might go further than mere praise and say that if Yeats had not been one of the greatest poets of the time through which he lived, he would have been its greatest charlatan. No actor of Yeats's long day (not even Sir Henry Irving) ever played a rôle with a more luxurious show of temperament and delight than the Yeatsian performance behind a mask; and here, as always, when we are surprised by some fresh turn of true ingeniousness, we cannot help but admire the brilliant display of energy and art by which he evaded the pitfalls of his fondest imitators. One enjoys the skill with which he acquired even the latest devices of his youngest contemporaries, including Messrs. W. H. Auden and Stephen Spender, and yet retained authority, choosing for himself the center of the stage.

It is with these reservations that one attempts to discriminate between the dramatic gesture and the poetic realities of Yeats's last appearances, between Yeats's love of the histrionic manner for its own sake and the genuine choice of a mask his daemon sought to wear. In the years between 1928 and 1939, it was all too plain that Yeats's earlier identities with William Blake and with Mallarmé had become shop-worn and that the mask of Shelley had long been tossed aside; and here it should be confessed that these impersonations were far less successful than the young Irishman's ability to assume the personae of the Gaelic myth; and though Yeats never relinquished the touchstones of what he conceived to be Blake's mysteries, extending their power in his latter years to adaptations of the *Upanishads*, he abandoned the gaudy trappings of a Blake revived and costumed by the Pre-Raphaelites for those of that "dirty old man," "that horrible spirit" who had been St. Patrick's most notorious Dean.

Even to the casual eye, the elder Yeats's identity with Swift is not without its own contrasts and denials. In re-reading Yeats's prose, one soon learns to distrust the flourish with which he introduced evocative, and sometimes semi-esoteric names, each name accompanied by that touch of rhetoric (borrowed from Walter Pater who had been his godfather in prose) which is at once the mark of a true style as well as the mannerism which always threatens to destroy it. He seemed always to have loved great names for their own sake, but his particular fondness was reserved for those that carried weight within a world of Anglo-Irish culture; he spoke of Helen and Pythagoras, Oisin and Leda, Christ and Cuchulain, Plotinus and Solomon, and against these he balanced another set of names and associations: Ibsen and Mr. G. B. Shaw, Madame Blavatsky and J. M. Synge, Fabian socialism and French Symbolism, Lionel Johnson and Mr. Ezra Pound—with this list of names in mind one becomes aware that no modern poet has inhabited or walked through so many schools and movements to his own advantage. In recognizing Yeats's intention to wear the mask of Swift, one must not look for signs of an absolute consistency; nor should one expect to find a literal analogy that would yield a comparison of *Gulliver's Travels* with the major poems of Yeats's last decade. The true identity is at once more subtle and more obvious, and the first (perhaps unconscious) step in that direction came as early as 1926 with the writing of the third section of *The Tower*:

> It is time that I wrote my will;
> I choose upstanding men
> That climb the streams until
> The fountain leap, and at dawn
> Drop their cast at the side
> Of dripping stone; I declare
> They shall inherit my pride,
> The pride of a people that were
> Bound neither to Cause nor to State
> Neither to slaves that were spat on,
> Nor to the tyrants that spat,
> The people of Burke and Grattan
> That gave, though free to refuse—
> Pride, like that of the morn,
> When the headlong light is loose.
> Or that of the fabulous horn,
> Or that of the sudden shower
> When all streams are dry,
> Or that of the hour
> When the swan must fix his eye
> Upon a fading gleam
> Float out upon a long
> Last reach of glittering stream
> And there sing his last song.

The presence, the heritage that Yeats recalled to mind was of Protestant, Anglo-Irish, eighteenth century Dublin, and in terms of that heritage he was about to write his will; and, as we shall soon discover, the line included the names of Swift and Goldsmith as well as those of Burke and Grattan, running forward in time to welcome and embrace the memories of Charles Stewart Parnell and Roger Casement. This line, however inclusive it may seem, is a road that does not permit excursions into the far sea lanes of *Gulliver's Travels*, nor into the writing cabinets and dossiers of Queen Anne's court, nor does it reveal the secret of India's forest philosophers so artfully hidden between the leaves of the *Upanishads*, but down that very road one readily unearths the long neglected verses of Dean Swift. It has been frequently observed that distances in time have little meaning in the streets of Dublin or on narrow highways in provincial Ireland; Dublin's eighteenth century speech and architecture, and in the provinces beyond the English pale, the shades of Druid seers and heroes share an equal martyrdom with Christian saints and victims of political misfortune. Even the merest glance at James Joyce's *Finnegans Wake* uncovers the rich and closely woven texture of an Irish past and present; heroes of lost centuries have a persistent, continuous, contemporaneous life within the fabric, so in the elder Yeats's discovery of Swift, the fruitful years of Swift's deanship at St. Patrick's seem at a mere arm's length from twentieth century O'Connell Street in Dublin.

Another indication of how variously alive that fabric was in Yeats's memory is generously stated in Mr. J. A. Symons's article *Wilde at Oxford* (*Horizon*, April, 1941). In speaking of John Pentland Mahaffy, called "The Admirable Crichton" of Trinity College (and who was one of Wilde's lecturers at Trinity), Mr. Symons wrote:

Above all his hobbies he prized what he called the art of the conversation. It was an "art" for which Dublin in the seventies provided an ample field of exercise, for the eighteenth century still survived in the Irish capital, and not only because the noble houses of Merrion Square and its neighborhood were occupied by men who could afford an eighteenth century lavishness of hospitality. Socially Dublin was more compact, and yet more inclusive than London then; it was dominated, not by an aristocracy rich enough to hold itself out of contact with the middle class, nor an aloof legendary Queen, but by the Vice Regal Court and its garrison of younger sons, who fraternized more or less on terms of equality with the Protestant ascendancy of law, medicine, church and university. Large dinner parties were a daily occurrence; they formed a stage on which any man of character might make his mark.

Among other things, one realizes here why Yeats's admiration for the mercurial Oscar Wilde was never broken —and why, though ruins and shades of the eighteenth century were still to be found in Dublin's streets sixty years later, the scene had grown comparatively dull and dirty. Although much remained of Yeats's youth, the glittering days of the Viceregal court were gone, and following them, the excitements and the diversions of the Gaelic Renaissance had also paled; the first World War (to say the least) had left his mark on Dublin and all Ireland: The Abbey Theatre was not what it had been; the semi-communist Irish Republicans were among the newest heroes, and there was reason enough for elder men of Anglo-Irish derivation, particularly those who had long memories, to identify themselves with images of bitterness and of loss.

Granting all this, one might still ask the question: Where does Swift come in? Why among the many masks through which Yeats spoke does the mask of Swift assume particular importance? From another source than those that

I have mentioned we begin to arrive at an answer through Mr. J. M. Hone's witty and intelligent appraisal of Yeats's politics; speaking of the time when Yeats served his term as a senator in Cosgrave's government, following the Irish "Troubles" of 1916-1921, Mr. Hone recalls a story of how Yeats replied to those who asked him the name of his political party. Was he an old Parnellite? Was he a Republican? Was it up Cosgrave and down De Valera? Yeats said calmly: "I am a Whig"—and laughter, derision, and confusion followed his remark. But the value of the joke which associated Senator William Butler Yeats with the Protestant landowning aristocracy in Ireland had more than a touch of Yeats's customary shrewdness in it; it brought back to mind memories of Dean Swift's political ironies, and with it the same quality of fear and distrust that unseated Swift at the court of Queen Anne when the Duchess of Somerset had but to whisper the word "atheist" and the would-be councilor of the Queen's ministers was exiled to the Deanery of St. Patrick's. Again Yeats had prepared himself (and perhaps the end in view was still unconscious) for the rôle of Swift in twentieth century Dublin; and, so far as Yeats was concerned, the part carried with it no direct or immediate political responsibilities; he was left free to modify the rôle, however, whenever he chose, for the lines to be spoken were too difficult, too harsh, too abstract for Yeats's Dublin contemporaries—it required a true act of poetic imagination to revive the bold, coarse-fibered image of Swift's personality on the Abbey stage in November, 1930.

In the introduction to his play, *The Words Upon the Window Pane*, Yeats wrote:

What shall occupy our imagination? We must, I think, decide among . . . three ideas of national life: that of Swift;

142

that of a great Italian of his day; that of modern England. If the Garrets and the Cellars listen I may throw light upon the matter, and I hope if all the time I seem to be thinking of something else I shall be forgiven. I must speak of things that come out of the common consciousness, where every thought is like a bell with many echoes. . . . Now I read Swift for months together, Burke and Berkeley less often but always with excitement, and Goldsmith lures and waits. I collect materials for my thought and work, for some of my identification of my beliefs with the nation itself, of its own permanent form, in that one Irish century that escaped from darkness and confusion, I seek an image of the modern mind's discovery of itself. I would that our fifteenth, sixteenth, or even our seventeenth century had been the clear mirror, but fate decided against us. . . . Swift haunts me; he is always just around the corner.

"Swift haunts me"—the phrase reminds one of the way Swift haunts the first page of *Finnegans Wake*, for Swift is a demi-myth of Irish consciousness, a name, a legend in itself as well as the author of the *Drapier Letters*. One may well wonder how Yeats spent "months together" reading Swift; we know from the introduction to *The Words upon the Window Pane* that he read the Fourth Drapier Letter and the *Discourse of the Contest and Dissensions Between the Nobles and the Commons in Athens and Rome*, a Whig document that contained a definition of three tyrannies, the One, the Few and the Many—and what is even more important, we know that he had also reread Swift's poetry. We can well understand how the unsolved mysteries of Swift's relationships to Vanessa and Stella stimulated the love of mystery for its own sake in Yeats's imagination, mysteries, by the way, that are as intractable as the problem of Hamlet's melancholy, and which offer an excuse for reinterpretation every time

Shakespeare's play makes its reappearance on the stage. Yeats's particular interest in the question: Was Swift mad? is of the same quality that marked his pursuit of Swedenborg which he followed with delight for so many years; the importance here was that he rediscovered a mystery in eighteenth century Dublin, and that in his effort to reinterpret it, he was led to a reading of Swift's *Verses to Vanessa* and *Stella's Birthday Poems*. Even in Dublin, where the memories of Swift have greater vitality than in any other place on earth, a rereading of his poetry carries with it the charm of verse that has been neglected; one had to seek out the poems in eighteenth century editions, and that semi-esoteric search alone would insure Yeats's interest for many "months together."

Thanks to Mr. Harold William's definitive edition of *The Poems of Jonathan Swift* we need not speculate too darkly upon the nature of Yeats's reading which prepared him for the performance of his last impressive rôle. The poems themselves bring to light the complexities of Swift's relationship to Queen Anne's court, to his friends in London, to Sir William Temple's excellent library (where the young Swift completed his literary education), to the Irish people, to politics in general, to Stella and Vanessa—and (which is perhaps the most important relationship of all) the relationship of Swift to his own verse.

Here one remembers Dr. Johnson's telling of the story how Dryden remarked: "Cousin Swift, you will never be a poet"; and in rereading the strained and lifeless *Pindaric Odes* inscribed to Sir William Temple, to King William and to the Athenian Society which young Swift wrote and Dryden read, we tend to believe that the elder poet's harsh-sounding judgment seems singularly mild. Until Swift grew to active manhood the writing of verse remained one of the larger elements in his complex of frustrations; in the presence of metrical numbers his imagination, his wit, his intelligence turned to stone, the lines of verse falling heavily across the page, spent and inert. The frequently quoted lines:

> My hate, whose lash just heaven has long decreed
> Shall on a day make sin and folly bleed;

were written at the age of twenty-six and lie hidden in an incredibly dull and abstracted series of couplets addressed *To Mr. Congreve*. It was not until Swift reached the age of forty-one that he wrote his first true poem, his second version of *Baucis and Philemon, Imitated, From the Eighth Book of Ovid*. Even the first version of the poem, written two years earlier, seems to have broken the spell of dullness which hung over him as he wrote verse, and it is significant that he broke the spell by discarding his attempts to write heroic verse. Swift adapted the story of a peasant's hut transformed into a shrine to a lively scene in Kent, the peasant's cottage changed into a village church, but this was no mere imitation of Ovid's *Baucis;* the fire, the inspiration that Swift had caught and adapted to his own use was the coarse, homely vein in Ovid which gave certain passages in his *Metamorphoses* an air of mock innocence and mock heroic charm, and it was at this point that Ovid closely resembled Plautus, which sharply differentiated his work from the larger and more richly elaborated structures of Virgil's *Aeneid* as well as the urban and polished brilliance of Horace's *Augustan Odes*. (And here, in a parenthesis, we need not forget the elder Yeats's desire to identify his work with the coarser fibers of Irish life, of which the rewriting of his poem *The Dedication to a Book of Stories Selected from the Irish Novelists* in the 1933 edition of his *Collected Poems* is a noteworthy example:

145

I also bear a bell-branch full of ease.

I tore it from green boughs winds tore and tossed
Until the sap of summer had grown weary!
I tore it from the barren boughs of Eire,
That country where a man can be so crossed;
Can be so battered, badgered and destroyed
That he's a loveless man. . . .

In these lines, the image of Swift's hand guiding Yeats's is all too clear.) The next twenty years of Swift's activity in writing verse, roughly, the years 1719 to 1739, relieved the burden of his own inadequacy in the composition of poetry. He had found a poetic style in which he could be master; it was a style in which the lively, almost anti-poetic wealth of realistic detail anticipated the narrative poetry of George Crabbe. Although the brief *A Description of the Morning* and *A Description of a City Shower* were exceptions to the rule, his characteristic verse form followed the metrics of Butler's *Hudibras;* it was a form peculiarly suited to his temperament, and as he adapted it to his own needs, he could resume it or shake it off with all the ease of wearing an old, comfortable and somewhat dirty dressing gown. Rather than seeming to be an overly strict or inhibiting discipline, the rhyming couplets gave him freedom to exercise his wit on a dull morning, to vent his anger, or to pay tribute to a friend.

Perhaps it is not too much to say that Yeats sought for a like freedom in his latter years, a freedom to use a vigorous masculine speech in verse with the same air that the aristocrat always meets the peasant on common ground—for both have always been outside the circle embracing middle-class society, since one is as much above the law as the other is below it. Here one remembers the miserable, dull-witted, brutish Irish peasants that enter Swift's mock pastorals, and with it one recalls a story told by Swift's publisher, George Faulkner, who described his author's method of correcting proofs for the Dublin edition of Swift's works in 1744. The proofs were read to two men-servants, "Which if they did not comprehend, he would alter and amend, until they understood it perfectly well, and then would say, 'This will do; for I write to the Vulgar, more than to the learned.'" There is a clear connection between the ironic wit of this story and another that Yeats wrote in a letter to Dorothy Wellesley, December 23, 1936:

Hate is a kind of "passive suffering" but indignation is a kind of joy. "When I am told that somebody is my brother protestant," said Swift, "I remember that the rat is a fellow creature"; that seems to me a joyous saying.

From this we move to other analogies between Swift's position in Dublin as Dean of St. Patrick's and Yeats's reputation in Ireland during the 1930's. Yeats's later poems, *The Tower, The Winding Stair, Words for Music Perhaps*, were better known in London and in New York than in the place where they were written and first saw light. He could almost say as Swift wrote to Charles Ford: "it is an infamous Case indeed to be neglected in Dublin when a man may converse with the best Company in London." In the broadest sense, he was again like Swift in that he seemed an apparition walking up and down familiar Dublin streets, exiled at home, a "Whig," slightly out of time and place, and like Swift he was both a Protestant interpreter of Ireland to a literate public in London, and the spokesman of an Anglo-Irish world to a nation of diffident, poverty-stricken, predominantly Roman Catholic people on his own soil.

147

If the mask of Swift was becoming to the years in which Yeats resumed his identity with the national life of the Irish people, one need not interpret all that both men had to say in terms of sexual impotence and personal, ungoverned loss of temper. Certain recent critics of both Yeats and Swift have found much to admire in rage and passion for their own sake; and they have frequently quoted Yeats's desire to be a "foolish, passionate old man" with the hope, perhaps, of emulating him when they themselves are "old and gray and full of sleep." But Swift, even at an early age, had learned to sublimate personal frustration in moral passion as he wrote . . . "the evil to be avoided is tyranny, that is to say, the summa imperii, or unlimited power solely in the hands of the one, the few, or the many . . ." and in his middle years, the defeat of his ambitions at Queen Anne's court found its cure in his identity with the unhappy Irish as he composed the *Drapier Letters*. While it would be absurd to assume that Yeats's "lust and rage" in his last years contained a proof of moral passion comparable to Swift's, or to claim that the sources of his rage were identical with those of the mask he wore, his *Saeva Indignatio* has a justification in his great gifts as a poet. Neither Yeats's *Blood and the Moon* nor Swift's masterpiece in verse, *On the Death of Dr. Swift*, is remembered solely because of the bitterness or rage some few of their lines imply: the latter survives because of Swift's observant, realistic eye and wit; and in Yeats's poem one realizes more than all else the power of his imaginative insight, as well as the appropriate uses of an imagery that lent distinction to his poetic style since the writing of *The Tower* in 1926. In the guise of Swift, Yeats well understood the rôle of seeming on occasion foolish, blasphemous, tortured, half-mad, holding in his heart, as a lighted candle, the frenzy of Dionysus. It is in this atmos-

148

phere and setting that one discovers the Crazy Jane songs, partly stimulated, of course, by Yeats's devotion to Spiritualism, that furthest, that last extreme of the Protestant attitude which develops from each man being his own priest and confessor to the logical conclusion (if logic can be applied to any aspect of religious faith) of being his own medium, echoing the voices of spirits from the dead.

In this connection, one might well ask the question: Who is Crazy Jane? And is she Ireland? Perhaps not, that would make too great a claim upon her identity. She is more accurately "of Ireland," quoting in her twentieth song a fragment of an old catch sung for at least six centuries on Irish soil:

> "*I am of Ireland,*
> *And the Holy Land of Ireland*
> *And time runs on,*" *cried she.*
> "*Come out of charity,*
> *Come dance with me in Ireland.*"

> One man, one man alone
> In that outlandish gear,
> One solitary man
> Of all that rambled there
> Had turned his stately head.

In *The Words upon the Window Pane*, Swift's presence on the stage is through the lips of Mrs. Henderson, a spiritualist medium, and Mrs. Henderson's control, Lulu, speaks of "that bad old man in the corner," who is Swift, and of the young lady who through Lulu's eyes is in fancy dress costume, "hair all in curls—all bent down on the floor near that old man with glasses." There is strong resemblance between the "solitary man" in outlandish gear and Lulu's Swift—he may not be the same man, but the resemblance is strong enough to establish a family relationship, and though Crazy Jane is not Vanessa, her solitary man will not dance with her no more than Swift yields to the demands of Vanessa's love. The dramatic action of both scenes is the same. The solitary man replies to Crazy Jane:

> "The fiddlers are all thumbs,
> Or the fiddle-string accursed,
> The drums and the kettledrums
> And the trumpets all are burst,
> And the trombone," cried he,
> "The trumpet and the trombone,"
> And cocked a malicious eye,
> "But time runs on, runs on."

As we keep in mind the solitary man's refrain "But time runs on, runs on," his family resemblance to Swift does not diminish in the rereading of *Stella's Birthday* written in 1724—that admirable poem compounded of masculine malice, wit, grace, tenderness, and love:

> Beauty and Wit, too sad a truth,
> Have always been confin'd to Youth:
> The God of Wit, and Beauty's Queen,
> He Twenty-one and She Fifteen:
> No Poet ever sweetly sung,
> Unless he were like *Phoebus*, young;
> Nor ever Nymph inspir'd to Rhyme,
> Unless, like *Venus*, in her Prime.
> At Fifty-six, if this be true,
> Am I a Poet fit for you?
> Or at the Age of Forty-three,
> Are you a Subject fit for me?
> Adieu bright Wit, and radiant Eyes;
> You must be grave, and I be wise.

150

Our Fate in vain we would oppose,
But I'll be still your Friend in Prose:
Esteem and Friendship to express,
Will not require Poetic Dress;
And if the Muse deny her Aid
To have them *sung* they may be *said*.

But, *Stella*, say, what evil Tongue
Reports you are no longer young?
That *Time* sits with his Scythe to mow
Where erst sate *Cupid* with his Bow;
That half your Locks are turn'd to Grey;
I'll ne'er believe a Word they say.
'Tis true, but let it not be known,
My Eyes are somewhat dimmish grown;
For Nature, always in the Right,
To your Decays adapts my sight,
And Wrinkles undistinguish'd pass,
For I'm asham'd to use a Glass;
And till I see them with these Eyes
Whoever says you have them, lyes.

No Length of Time can make you quit
Honour and Virtue, Sense and Wit,
Thus you may still be young to me,
While I can better *hear* than *see*;
Oh, ne'er may Fortune shew her Spight,
To make me *deaf*, and mend my *Sight*.

To change the metaphor back from sight to hearing, surely "The fiddlers are all thumbs,/Or the fiddle-string accursed"—but who, again, is Crazy Jane? While her relationships to the men of whom she speaks place her by broad analogy within the same world that witnessed the Irish "Troubles" of 1916-1921 and the years of De Valera's rise to power, she is clearly not Stella, nor of the line to which Burke and Grattan belonged. She is of that underworld that Burns saw when he wrote *The Jolly Beggars*, and her language has a half-romantic, half-neoclassic turn of eloquence. Since Yeats's reading, like all of Anglo-Irish Dublin's, always returned with a fixed, yet casual, eye upon the literature of the eighteenth century, we need not be surprised to find another Crazy Jane in Tomkin's obscure anthology of *Poems on Various Subjects*, London, 1804. Her author was M. G. Lewis, Esq. M. P. and under her name we find these lines:

> Why, fair maid, in ev'ry feature,
>   Are such signs of fear express'd?
> Can a wand'ring wretched creature
>   With such terrors fill thy breast?
> Do my frenzied looks alarm thee?
>   Trust me, sweet—thy fears are vain
> Not for Kingdoms would I harm thee,
>   Shun not then poor Crazy Jane.
>
> Dost thou weep to see my anguish?
>   Mark me! and avoid my woe;
> When men flatter, sigh and languish,
>   Think them false—I found them so:
> For I lov'd—Oh! so sincerely.
>   None could ever love again:
> But the youth I lov'd so dearly,
>   Stole the wits of Crazy Jane.
>
> .   .   .   .   .
>
> Now forlorn and broken-hearted,
>   And with frenzied thoughts beset;
> On that spot where last we parted,
>   On that spot where first we met.

> Still I sing my love-lorn ditty,
> Still I slowly pace the plain;
> While each passerby in pity
> Cries—God help thee, Crazy Jane!

Following poor Jane's "frenzied looks" what an excellent companion she makes for "Swift beating on his breast in sibylline frenzy blind/Because the heart in his blood-sodden breast had dragged him down into mankind"!—and with her cry through Yeats's lips, "All things remain in God," the scene rounds to completion upon a darkening stage.

In recreating the figure of Crazy Jane, Yeats also displayed his greatest contradiction in assuming the rôle of Swift in twentieth century Ireland. If Jane's unhappy plight recalls Ireland's past and present—and even now, perhaps a large part of Ireland's future—it also recalls the familiar burdens of Thomas Moore's *Irish Melodies*. Readers of Yeats's early poems, particularly those who remember *The Lake Isle of Inisfree*, can recognize at once the impure, almost maudlin strain that Yeats had inherited from "The harp that once through Tara's halls/The soul of music shed." That Yeats in his latter years was able to go behind the *Irish Melodies*, tracing their music to a relatively pure, less tarnished source, is, of course, among the signs of his true genius. But if one reads those poems of the Crazy Jane cycle that are less successful than the best, a note of pathos and ill-timed heroics sounds all too clearly on the ear. The obvious flaw in Yeats's performance of a great rôle was his inability to see the mock-heroic aspects of Swift's life and work, the mock hero whose shade overhears the gossip of Queen Anne's court in the verses *On the Death of Dr. Swift*. No one in his right senses would lay great claims for Swift's ability as a lyric poet, so here in

Yeats's disability to realize fully the mock-heroic character of Swift's verse as well as the moral passion which ran beneath its lines, we find Yeats at his weakest, attempting to transform an essentially ironic rôle into terms of tragedy.

If Yeats's identity with Swift cannot be held responsible for the best of all his work (a list which should include *In Memory of Major Robert Gregory, An Irish Airman Foresees His Death, Sailing to Byzantium,* and *The Tower* itself, as well as a half-dozen poems selected from *The Winding Stair*) the mask helped to sustain his energy as he approached death through the distractions of old age. Swift's late maturity was in itself a heartening example, and the vigor of Swift's intellect was in truth "the strength that gives our blood and state magnanimity of its own desire," an abstract, moral passion that Yeats did not possess, but could, on occasion, simulate with the superior graces of an accomplished actor. In *The Words upon the Window Pane* one hears Yeats's Swift echoing the words of Job and Sophocles' chorus from *Oedipus at Colonus:*

Never to have lived is best, ancient writers say;
Never to have drawn the breath of life, never to have
    looked into the light of day,

as his will overpowers Mrs. Henderson, shouting, "Perish the day on which I was born!"—which remains, even at its best, an uncontrolled mixture of tragi-comic associations. The play is not a tragedy, yet it points the direction, if one remembers Yeats's translation of *Oedipus at Colonus,* of his furthest reach toward an understanding of a tragic situation in human life, and for Yeats it seemed to be (or rather, this is the impression his play leaves upon the reader) a statement of the purge that relieves the terrors of old age. For the rest, we hear the remote, perhaps the very last, intonations of Yeats's voice through the mask of

Swift in *Under Ben Bulben*, which Dorothy Wellesley tells us was first given the uninspired title *His Convictions:*

> Irish poets, learn your trade,
> Sing whatever is well made,
> Scorn the sort now growing up
> All out of shape from toe to top,
> Their unremembering hearts and heads
> Base-born products of base beds.
> Sing the peasantry, and then
> Hard-riding country gentlemen,
> The holiness of monks, and after
> Porter-drinkers' randy laughter;
> Sing the lords and ladies gay
> That were beaten into clay
> Through seven heroic centuries;
> Cast your mind on other days. . . .

The verse is not Yeats at his best; the metrics rattle onward with few pauses to their stop until they arrive at the truly excellent:

> Cast a cold eye
> On life, on death.
> Horseman, pass by!

Yeats had outworn the mask with his death; the play was over and the curtains drawn.

ON D. H. LAWRENCE AND HIS POSTHUMOUS
REPUTATION

"I SHALL live just as blithely, unbought and unsold," wrote D. H. Lawrence in 1925. And in this remark there is a note of prophecy that describes the curious nature of his survival during the half dozen years following his death. Perhaps none of the earlier objections to his work has been removed since 1930, yet his influence has endured in the kind of fame that Matthew Arnold perceived in Shelley's reputation which was both legend and literature and both "ideal" and "ridiculous." Much of Lawrence's ardent pamphleteering is now outmoded. And nothing seems to have grown so clearly out of fashion in a few short years than Lawrence's specific lectures on sex and obscenity. To-day they seem to have gone to the same place reserved in memory for the events of early postwar Europe and America. Yet even in his most perishable writing the character of his influence remains.

However and wherever Lawrence is reread, whether in scattered posthumous papers, or in the poems, short stories, or in the novels, it is the speaking voice that is heard clearest and remembered. We then recall Lawrence's letters, which seem always to renew at each date line a briefly interrupted conversation and with them we remember Mr. David Garnett's little sketches of how he worked: writing as he cooked his meals or sat in one corner of a room while others talked, writing as he unpacked boxes and suitcases, writing almost as he moved and breathed, as though the traveling of his hand across paper were the very reflex of his being. Surely, this prodigality was "art for my sake" and was the visible power of the thing he called his "demon" which is to say that much of it was scarcely art at all. Artfulness was sometimes deftly concealed within the larger rhythm of conversation; and sometimes his "demon" was called upon to gratify an urgently explicit demand of form: These moments are identified with the writing of *Sons and Lovers* as well as the writing of a half dozen poems and three or four short stories, but in the rest of everything he wrote the more flexible rule of "art for my sake" was applied and satisfied.

Lawrence, of course, was by no means unaware of what was happening; he had read his critics and matched his wit with theirs:

> For me, give me a little splendour, and I'll leave perfection to the small fry. . . . Ugh, Mr. Muir, think how horrible for us all, if I were perfect! or even if I had "perfect" gifts! Isn't splendour enough for you, Mr. Muir? Or do you find the peacock more "perfect" when he is moulting and has lost his tail, and therefore isn't so exaggerated, but is more "down to normal"?—For "perfection" is only one of "the normal" and the "average" in modern thought.

How well he knew that the image of the peacock's tail would fill the reader's eye; and there in the image itself, he had uncovered a fragment of the "splendor" he had sought, and with an eloquent gesture, passed it over to the reader. It was as though he had been saying: Mr. Muir has given me bread and I give you cake. My transformation of Mr. Muir's gift, dear reader, is your reward for reading me. This answer was always Lawrence's reply to authority, whether the authority was the Evangelist, preaching from a Nottinghamshire pulpit, or Roman law concealed within the new laws of the Fascisti, whether it was the British censor or Mr. Muir. But he was always least fortunate whenever he attempted to answer that authority directly: his ingenuity lay in the art of improvised distraction. And in distracted argument he was never more successful than in his reply to Mr. Muir.

With Lawrence's rejection of the average man came his distrust of the society around him: "Only the people we don't meet are the 'real' people," he wrote in *Jimmy and the Desperate Woman*—and his "real" people were "the simple, genuine, direct, spontaneous, unspoilt souls," which, of course, were not to be found among the people Lawrence saw on city streets, not in "London, New York, Paris," for "in the bursten cities, the dead tread heavily through the muddy air," and in each face he saw the same stigmata Blake had witnessed, "marks of weakness, marks of woe." These were his average, "normal" people, branded by service in the World War like Captain Herbertson in *Aaron's Rod*, mutilated by war and sanctified by bourgeois wealth like Chatterley, malformed by ignorance and poverty like the Nottinghamshire miner, or tricked and defeated like the American Indian, "Born with a caul, a black membrane over the face." And as Lawrence traveled, he saw the same disease spread over half the earth—and he was not to be identified with any of that kind, the meek, the humble, or the dead. Though the physical resemblance to Lawrence's speaking voice may be traced throughout his novels, through Paul Morel, Lilly of *Aaron's Rod* or Mellors of *Lady Chatterley's Lover*, he was happiest in another kind of personality; and the image of the bird was best: The mythical phoenix, the peacock, or the Tuscan nightingale. To defend the nightingale (as well as himself) against the "plaintive anthem" of John Keats's *Ode*, he wrote:

How astonished the nightingale would be if he could be made to realize what sort of answer the poet was answering his song. He would fall off the bough with amazement.

Because a nightingale, when you answer him back, only shouts and sings louder. Suppose a few other nightingales pipe up in the neighboring bushes—as they always do. Then the blue-white sparks of sound go dazzling up to heaven. And suppose you, mere mortal, happen to be sitting on the shady bank having an altercation with the mistress of your heart, hammer and tongs, then the chief nightingale swells and goes at it like Caruso in the Third Act—simply a brilliant, bursting frenzy of music, singing you down, till you simply can't hear yourself speak to quarrel.

Of course, the nightingale was the very thing Lawrence wished himself to be, the thing apart from the quarreling couple on the shady bank and his "art for my sake" had for its model the work of a creature who

. . . sings with a ringing, pinching vividness and a pristine assertiveness that makes a mere man stand still. A kind of brilliant calling and interweaving of glittering exclamation such as must have been heard on the first day of creation.

This was the splendor that was Lawrence's great concern, the "bursting frenzy of music" that emanated from a source within the body, and was itself the body, the physical being of a living creature. The lack of that physical force was his definition of modern tragedy, and it was the same emptiness he had witnessed in the lives of the civilized people who surrounded him. In that self-pitying, sad, silent company he had seen the image of Paul Morel, his early self of *Sons and Lovers*.

159

. . . left in the end naked of everything, with the drift toward death . . . It's the tragedy of thousands of young men in England.

But Lawrence's instructions to live the splendid life always had the tendency to oversimplify the cure for complex (and human) silences and fears. They were all too much like telling friends and neighbors to be natural, to "go be a man." His work had all the skill and all the confident lack of knowledge of one who had carefully trained himself to conduct an orchestra by ear. Throughout Lawrence's verse and prose a dominant rhythm persists above loose phrasing and verbal monotony; his ear had been trained to catch the idiomatic inflection of English speech, avoiding always the outmoded rhythms of literary usage. In this respect his work shares the vitality of Whitman's verse and Melville's prose, and like theirs it contains the same self-taught art that controlled its imagery.

Even the most casual reader of Lawrence will soon become aware of how deliberately he avoided the urban image and how through prose and verse there is a literal predominance of "birds, beast, and flowers." And as their number increases, how tropical they seem, and we remember that his need for physical well-being followed the hot course of the sun. But it is characteristic of Lawrence's imagery that its action remains suspended in utter darkness or in the full flood light of noon; and though it is frequently breathing and alive, it seldom extends its force to an actual climax. How many of his images start bravely and end in helplessness, as though they could not carry the burden of their swelling heat and color to move elsewhere! And this same helplessness enters the majority of his many poems, all incomplete, all lacking in the distinction of verbal action to give them motion and finality. How many of his novels end with the promise of a life beyond them yet to be fulfilled in the next novel, perhaps, but for the moment still unwritten! Only in *Sons and Lovers*, and in a few of the short stories do we find a definite space of time and action brought to an ultimate conclusion—only in these and in three or four of the *Last Poems*. The rest of his work leans heavily into the future, as though the next page to be written would complete the large design of which his fragments were pencil sketches from the living model.

I suspect that this very characteristic of incompleted action is responsible for the air of expectancy which welcomed the publication of each posthumous volume of letters, stories, poems, essays, or incidental papers. Lawrence in death seemed still in flight around the globe and it has been difficult to think of him as a middle-aged writer dying nerveless and exhausted in a sunlit room in Southern France. The biographies of Lawrence, his self-imposed exile from England, the disorder among camp-followers of the Lawrence household may be used as sources for a facile parallel to Shelley's death and the legends which grew out of it. But how eagerly Lawrence would have hated Shelley and would have cheerfully denied all he had written, and did in fact answer his *To a Skylark* in the same language in which he replied to Keats's nightingale:

"Hail to thee, blithe Spirit!—bird thou never wert." Why should he insist on the bodilessness of beauty when we cannot know of any save embodied beauty? Who would wish that the skylark were not a bird, but a spirit? If the whistling skylark were a spirit, then we should all wish to be spirits. Which were impious and flippant.

We need not stop to consider the flaws in Lawrence's heavy-footed questioning, for in this reply there is implied an entire century's increased distrust of Platonic reasoning.

Between Shelley and Lawrence arose the shadow of Nietzsche's Zarathustra, who said as he descended from the mountain:

To blaspheme the earth is now the dreadfulest sin. . . . Man is a rope stretched between the animal and the Superman. . . . Aye, for the game of creating, my brethren, there is needed a holy Yea unto Life. . . .

Lawrence's great error, of course, was to echo the sound of Zarathustra's warning without clear knowledge of the myth from which Nietzsche's hero had sprung, and lacking this knowledge he could not stride into another world that lay beyond good and evil. The literary heritage of the early nineteenth century had come down to him by way of Herman Melville and Walt Whitman. As he entered the latter phases of his career, traces of Whitman's eloquence spread throughout his writing, yet he was always to reject Whitman's democracy with uneasy violence. Whatever was to remain revolutionary in Lawrence's thinking was something that resembled philosophic anarchy. In a recently discovered paper, *Democracy*, written in 1923, he used Whitman as his text, in both praise and blame, to reiterate his distrust of a bourgeois democracy and its possession of property. His rejection of authority included a consistent denial of Marx as well as Plato, of Aquinas as well as Judaism and all law of church and state.

Yet in this wide negation of authority lies one secret of his influence with a younger generation of postwar writers. To deny bourgeois authority and to leave England was to break down the barriers of class and national prejudice that had seemed impassable before 1918, or rather, had remained unbroken for nearly a hundred years. He had survived many forms of British bourgeois hostility which brought with them the lack of a large reading pub-

162

lic, persecution from the War Office, and the action of the British censor as well as charges of religious heresy. And there was ample evidence to convict him on any or all of these charges of public disfavor. His reply was that he alone remained alive in a dead world, a world in which the memory of its millions killed in a World War had spread the shadow of mass murder as well as lonely suicide over the furthest reaches of Anglo-Saxon civilization. And when his own death came, he made his own choices in preparation for it, convincing himself and those who read him that he had chosen the path of stilled and dark waters into oblivion.

Almost with his last breath he was to say, "For man the vast marvel is to be alive. For man, as for flower, and beast and bird . . ." and this reassurance in the goodness of physical being from someone whose self-taught and imperfect gifts alone sustained his eloquence, created a hero for a generation that feared the stillness of its own despair. It is not without perception that Mr. T. S. Eliot as well as others have read the warning of disease in Lawrence's heresies of behavior and craftsmanship. We know only too well his many failures, and among them we learn his refusal to abide by the truth of his observation in writing a brilliant analysis of Baron Corvo's *Hadrian the Seventh:* "A man must keep his earnestness nimble to escape ridicule." Yet his insight was never more profound nor more direct than when he associated Whitman with his own name, for it is through the work of Lawrence that the younger men in his generation of British writers have learned the actual significance of Whitman's enduring reputation. Like Whitman, Lawrence left behind him no model of technique that would serve to crystallize the style of prose or poetry in those who followed him. Lawrence's influence as a teacher was irrevocably bad; surely his literal imitators, like Horace Traubel's discipleship of Whitman, illustrate the master's flaws until their burlesque becomes so clear that pity or contempt deflects all criticism. Such imitation is the pathetic attempt to reproduce the absence of form, as though the devoted student had amputated his arm to simulate the sensation of his master's missing hand. Lawrence's real strength, like his invisible presence living "blithely, unbought and unsold," is explicit only in the combined force of his legend with a small selection from his prolific work of less than twenty years, and from these fragments we learn again how vividly he revived the memory of the maker in English literature, restoring the moment of vision and insight as a mark of genius in English prose and poetry.

ON HISTORY AND HISTORIANS AND THE
PROSE OF DR. WILLIAM CARLOS WILLIAMS

"HISTORY, history!" says Dr. William Carlos Williams, and then with brilliant asperity continues, "We fools, what do we know or care?"

The quantum of irony in Dr. Williams's remark, though clear enough, should be carefully considered, and in the way I read it, it might well be taken as a warning. History is a humiliating subject for any man to think of knowing: and however much, however little we know of it, we always care, and that is where the trouble is likely to begin. The desire to know history is a near relative of the desire to know truth, and that is where, for most of us, a pit lies waiting. It is a deep pit, overlaid with an innocent branch or two, cut down from a near-by tree, and among a scattering of wilted leaves, there are easily plucked twigs and tamed, resistant grasses. At its sides and at an attractive distance, one also finds rare specimens of jungle flora. It is a pretty place and only a very few of the so-called professional historians come back from it alive. For the moment I can remember the names of only three who came back whole: Herodotus, Edward Gibbon, and Henry Adams, and of these, Herodotus, being the eldest and most respectable, is best known as "the father of lies."

Perhaps, there has always been a great number of different kinds of people who were eager to think of themselves as historians. Perhaps, this was always so, but during the past few years, there seems to have been an increase of their published work; they seem to have become more vocal, more insistent that the field of history is theirs to have and to hold, and is in itself a proof of their authority to speak aloud. There it is, that deep pit, growing more inviting every day: and to it come engineers, and social workers, members of the D.A.R., and psychiatrists, economists and students of anthropology, newspaper men and politicians by the hundreds, research workers in the sciences, and, no doubt, an aviator or two. Executives of all kinds have come to it, from insurance company offices, from the Stock Exchange, from banks to overawe club banquets or trustee meetings or to deliver commencement-day addresses at schools and colleges. And in addition to all these, there are those many talkative members of a generation (of whom some write novels) who have a strong memory of what their grandfathers told them about the Civil War. The clearing in the jungle shines before them and they walk into it.

Of course, we have always known that history, like poetry, is an ancient trap laid for the credulous and literal-minded. This common knowledge has been abroad so long that we are apt to forget the obvious hint that only those who have imagination survive their fall from unhappy innocence. Many, and I would say, far, far too many, are still victims of that fall: good, earnest people who are maimed and battered, who are forced to carry on a half-existence, distrusted by their fellows and of continual embarrassment to their friends.

Nor is it enough to have convictions and a powerful will to interpret them. Here history most resembles truth, and however violent its events have been and however lively they still appear, its exterior seems almost passive, and certainly tempting, if not altogether calm. Here, it seems to be waiting for the strong man to claim it, to do whatever he pleases with it and to make it his own forever. To use history for their purposes alone is the common ambition of the politician and the political journalist, and some have done so, and have made that great pit yield great profits for them. But even here imagination has been translated into action, and when that happens politicians become statesmen and mere corporals become heroes—and here it is not what they do to history that matters, but what history does to them.

There must be imagination at work to discern the fabulae of history, to know their mutable faces, to know their language. Those who ignore them are sure to be lost at the deepest level of the pit. Their shrewdness is then known for the true stupidity that it is and always has been. They are the lost, the very lost, who are forgotten with remarkable ease and are unearthed only by industrious persons in libraries for whom the discovery of an unknown name may score a one-hundredth of a point toward a Ph.D.

It is in this relationship, between what is sometimes called fabulae and what is sometimes called fact, that the "historical imagination" plays its part. And here there has always been a long established kinship between the historical imagination and poetry. The serious historian of the ancient world is careful never to forget his Homer. He may discriminate among the fabulae that Homer has set before him, and in the course of his researches, he may reject a number of them. But there they are; and they happen to remain in a better state of preservation than the buried cities unearthed by archeologists. There is a particular kind of reality alive within them that will permit neither neglect nor violation: and in the reading and interpretation of history everything falls dead unless that reality is perceived. The truth of events as a cautious historian may come to

167

know it, and the meaning of that same truth to a people who have converted it into a common heritage demand a living, active synthesis. This is as true today as it always was, and the fabulae of American history, youthful and knowingly familiar as they may seem to some of us, are no exception to the rule.

One might almost say that the active fabulae of a human culture are the means through which it lives and grows. They enter deeply into the very idiom of national speech; their meanings shift as the spoken language changes. On this continent, they are "in the American grain" and it is humanly impossible to adopt an impartial, or what was once called a "scientific," attitude toward them. Science, as we have come to know it, is none too quiet in making its own discriminations, and shall we say it has its own signs, its own language by which its own truths are tested and modified? Shall we say that the imagination of a Willard Gibbs, whose language is abstract only to those who do not understand it, has its own nucleus of fabulae—or shall we call them the mathematical symbols of reality?

Our nationality which answers to the name, American, is neither at the center of a huge continent nor is it floating loosely around its East, West, and Tropical coast lines and harbors. It is a language, and it requires a particularly active and discerning imagination to keep pace with it and to speak it truly. Without knowing that language as well as the signs and symbols it employs, the would-be historian is almost helpless. Lacking that particular insight, the professional historian is in the same unfortunate position as that of the non-professionals who cross his field. He may contribute a formula or a theory toward a revaluation of history in general, but he will need someone at his side to translate it, some one to make it intelligible to Americans.

It is at this point that Dr. Williams's discovery of an

American heritage becomes important. His manner is almost aggressively non-professional and rightly so, for he is not here to record American history nor to give us a new sequence of events. He is here to present its signs and signatures, its backward glances, and by implication, its meanings for the future.

If I have misled some readers into thinking that *In the American Grain* is an historical textbook, or a book of essays in history, or a series of historical narratives, I wish to correct that impression before I go one word further. It is none of these. It is a source book of highly individual and radical discoveries, a book of sources, as one might say a river is a source of health to the fields and orchards through which it runs. And like that river in its uneven course, now quick in sunlight and now flowing to hidden roots of trees and flowers, the book has subterranean depths and turnings. I think it is not too much to say that this analogy also resembles its early reputation.

In the American Grain was first published in 1925 and before that date an early chapter appeared in *Broom*. I have no way of knowing how many people saw a few of its chapters in magazines or read the book, but I do know that as it fell slowly out of print, its reputation grew. I suspect that several other writers came upon it and kept the memory of its insights and the quality of its prose within the hidden chambers of their own knowledge and imagination. My immediate example is Hart Crane's *The Bridge* which was published five years later and which carried within it traces of the impression left upon those who first read *In the American Grain*. These traces are to be found throughout the poem: a fragment of Dr. Williams's quotation from Thomas Morton's *The New England Canaan* is reproduced on the half-title page of *Powhatan's Daughter* and like selections may be quickly recognized in the concluding pages of Dr. Williams's chapter on Columbus and in the closing stanzas of *Ave Maria*. Even the quotation from Edgar Poe's *The City in the Sea* (whose original title was significantly written as *The Doomed City*), "Death looks gigantically down," smolders in a half-line of *The Tunnel* and also appears in Dr. Williams's book, placed over "a dead world, peopled by shadows and silence, and despair. . . ." These similarities should not of course be read as plagiarisms, nor should we exaggerate their obvious claims to a relationship that exists between them and the publication of *In the American Grain*. The point is that Dr. Williams's book exerted an influence that rose from the subsoil of the time in which it was written, and like all work of highly original temper and spirit and clarity it survives the moment of its conception. In this respect the book has something of the same force that generates the work of others, the same brilliance, the same power to shed light in darkened places that we have learned to respect in Miss Marianne Moore's poetry and in Miss Gertrude Stein's *Three Lives*.

Another association that *In the American Grain* brings forcefully to mind is the period of critical impressionism in America, that hour in the 1920's when Sherwood Anderson published his notebooks and D. H. Lawrence's *Studies in Classic American Literature* were read. *In the American Grain*, though not resembling either, is of the same moment that lies behind a barrier of critical controversy in American letters dividing this moment from an hour when certain strength was derived from highly individual insights and convictions. A reaction against mere self-expression, mere sensitivity and feeling, came in with the disciples of what was then called Humanism. And against this movement came those who sought to clarify the direction that Vernon Louis Parrington had already taken. At this distance the quarrel which now seems older than its years, now also seems to have been one in which its two opposing factors united against a common enemy. The enemy was impressionistic thinking and activity, and in the heat of the moment, all work of personal identity and imagination became suspect. Without entering into the merits and abuses of the controversy, it should now be possible to look behind the dust raised in that hour. During the time of the rising quarrel, everything that had a personal exterior aroused fears and distrust of heresy and was therefore publicly ignored or attacked as the true heresy it was supposed to signify. Through these brief years *In the American Grain* shared something of the public obscurity that was intended to cover the remains of personal heresy and choice. Meanwhile, the book was kept intact for the discerning reader and as it may be read today, it retains its original coloring and a great measure of its purity.

What I have just said is another way of saying that certain recent beliefs and attitudes in criticism have begun to reverse themselves: although the mannerisms of impressionistic criticism have been properly discredited and should not be revived, it is now admitted that the writer cannot shift the very foundations of his beliefs without endangering the verbal truth of what he has to say. It had also been discovered that the raptures and ardors of sudden conversion to any cause, however valid the cause itself may be, seldom, if ever, revive the dying powers of imaginative insight and creation. Human growth is far too slow to admit violent denials of its immediate past, and writers, quite like other human beings, become inept and voiceless should they attempt to deny the continuity of their heritage.

Anyone who has read all of Dr. Williams's prose and verse becomes aware of its great ability to grow at its own pace. And if anyone is looking for the secret of its good health and the freedom it exerts within an individual speech and manner, it may be found in its determination to "stay at home," to accept the roots of its being and to grow slowly to its full maturity. This radical willingness to accept the limitations of normal growth has given Dr. Williams's work a quality that resembles an aspect of life itself; it is a kind of reality that absorbs its own mistakes and shortcomings and should be cited as an example of true well-being.

Dr. Williams has been referred to as being "sincere," but the difficult question of sincerity in art, which is too often confused with gossip or speculation concerning the personal or public behavior of the man who happens to be a writer, should be referred to the continuity of his imagination and the speech that gives it meaning. We cannot expect to answer so large a question to the satisfaction of everyone, and M. Paul Valéry has devoted no small degree of his fine intelligence to warn us of the dangers of considering it with any seriousness at all. Yet I believe that the more important difficulties of the question may arrive at a fruitful, if partial solution, by observing the triple unities of speech and imagination and emotion, and of their relationship to each other within a book.

One of the peculiarities of this question is its seeming lack of relevance to classical literatures: that is, it seems absurd to question the sincerity of Homer, of Sophocles, or of Aeschylus, or the authors of *The Palatine Anthology*. In these cases the relevance of the question seems all too clear and certainly naïve. What we have learned to respect in the remains of an ancient literature—and these however dimly they may be interpreted and translated—are its elements of unity. In instances where the authorship is obscure, we can at least distinguish between the language of

172

one period and that of another until at last we enter the world of the Middle Ages by way of Rome. The unities of time and of place in the poetic drama tended to strengthen the unities of speech and tradition—and a discernable continuity of ritual and moral attitude answers the question of sincerity before it rises to the surface of the reader's mind.

As we approach the writing of our own time, the question re-emerges in many forms, and however we try to dismiss or slide beyond it, it remains to stir our sense of guilt and to evaluate the writer's integrity. One hears the word "sincerity" used as a term of polite abuse as well as dubious praise: and to us its implications may mean no more than the writer is a good fellow of admirable intentions—give the poor dog the merits of sincerity and let his work be damned. It is sometimes futile to reply that the unintelligent, the insensible, the undiscerning, the unimaginative (if they are writers), are incapable of sincerity in what they write; their relationship to what they say is already compromised before they start; at best they are merely writing with half a voice and half an ear, and their beliefs rest upon such shallow ground that they are meaningless almost before we discover what they are. I suspect that the clear evidence of sincerity in Dr. Williams's work is no mere illusion created by his literary personality, nor do I believe that verbal continuity of *In the American Grain* is a fortunate accident. One cannot divorce its theme from the voice that speaks it; and even its lengthy quotations from *Poor Richard* and John Paul Jones derive their pertinence from Dr. Williams's entire scheme of presentation.

I also believe that Dr. Williams's theme, though for a separate reason, is no less dangerous than the desire to know history or a definition of sincerity which seems so necessary in describing the nature of his work. The old theme of America as a new world to be rediscovered at every turn has rather more than its full share of contradictions. The impulse to make all things new, to build new cities in a clearing of the forest, to abandon projects with the scaffolding in air, to move onward to another El Dorado is a familiar complex of the American tradition. It contains within it the sources of our wealth and poverty, our despair and hopefulness, and it is something that Herman Melville saw before him as he wrote:

> The Ancient of Days forever is young,
>   Forever the scheme of Nature thrives;
> I know a wind in purpose strong—
>   It spins *against* the way it drives.
> What if the gulfs their slimed foundations bare?
>   So deep must stones be hurled
> Whereon the throes of ages rear
>   The final empire and the happier world.

It is the "happier world" that seems so often to elude us and is the world Dr. Williams so frequently discovers on earth and not in heaven. To make these discoveries seem alive and new also implies the cheerful will to outface the dangers of a theme that grows too large for habitation, and too many writers have already lost themselves in that blue vault in which the images of rebirth and the sensations of becoming are reiterated with alarming regularity. One might almost say that our long-continued faith in "the American renaissance" is an habitual response to living on this continent, as though we waked each morning to find a new world still-born at our door. The faith contains so many apparitions of a dead new world that one is now tempted to respond to them with the same gesture which

174

was implied as John Webster's Duke of Calabria looked down at his dead sister:

Cover her face; mine eyes dazzle: she died young.

But Dr. Williams makes this discovery of his tradition with the insight of a man who walks into a brightly lighted room and there, for the first time, actually sees the things he has lived with all his life. He then makes his selection of what truly belongs to him and discards others; he repairs some pieces that have become chipped or broken, some he adapts to his immediate needs and some he leaves untouched—but all are endowed from this moment onward with the same qualities of suspense and animation that seem to enter an old house as it waits for the arrival of an heir or a new master.

As Dr. Williams wrote in his note on poetry which appeared in *The Oxford Anthology of American Literature:*

In my own work it has always sufficed that the object of my attention be presented without further comment. This in general might be termed the objective method . . . since the senses did not exist without an object for their employment all art is necessarily objective. It doesn't declaim or explain; it presents . . . Times change and forms and their meaning alter. . . . Their forms must be discovered in the spoken, the living language of their day.

Therefore, the earlier chapters of *In the American Grain* are rich in selection from original documents and the continuity of their separate statements is preserved by Dr. Williams's quickened adjustment of his own prose to their cadence and imagery.

Within this pattern of selection and commentary I find but one example that seems to betray the moment of time in which the book was written. During the 1920's the general feeling against Puritanism slipped into third gear and ran beyond control. The reasons for it are so well known that they deserve no further defense or contradiction. It is true that one whole side of Puritan culture represents a destructive element in the American tradition and something of its decadence was felt and recognized in Eugene O'Neill's *The Great God Brown*. In itself it contains the ambiguity of Melville's wind that "spins against the way it drives" and like the image of that wind it seems to stir hatreds and admirations that are both too vague and too large for hasty discrimination. I would say that Dr. Williams's choice of quotation from Cotton Mather echoes the usual cry against the Puritan without revealing the full character of Mather's genius. It contains too little hint of Mather's wit and administrative abilities, and scarcely anything at all of the imagination that created political parables with such memorable skill. Dr. Williams is on firmer ground when he writes of the Puritan "spirit" and its meaning:

And so they stressed the "spirit"—for what else could they do?—and this spirit *is* an earthly pride which they, prideless, referred to heaven and the next world. And for *this* we praise them, instead of for the one thing in them that was valuable: their tough littleness and the weight of many to carry through the cold; not their brokenness but their project of the great flower of which they were the seed.

So with an eye that is aware of the reality existing in the fabulae of history, even to the recording of Washington's famous "reputation for truthfulness," and with a fine perception of the hidden values of sincerity, that kind of truth that is best described in the qualities he attributes to Aaron

176

Burr, Dr. Williams creates an atmosphere that many Americans should recognize as home.

I leave the discovery of Dr. Williams's prose to his readers, yet I cannot resist the temptation to quote the two closing paragraphs of his chapter on Sir Walter Raleigh, for there are few examples in twentieth century writing equal to its lyricism:

> Sing, O Muse and say, there is spirit that is seeking through America for Raleigh: in the earth, the air, the waters, up and down, for Raleigh that lost man: seer who failed, planter who never planted, poet whose works are questioned, leader without command, favorite deposed—but one who yet gave title for his Queen, his England, to a coast he never saw but grazed alone with genius.

> Question him in hell, O Muse, where he has gone, and when there is an answer, sing and make clear the reasons that he gave for that last blow. Why did he send his son into that tropic jungle and not go himself, upon so dangerous an errand? And when the boy had died why not die too? Why England again and force the new King to keep his promise and behead him?

And there is no writer who has perceived the complex figure of Lincoln—whose very name seems always to evoke the worst of histrionic rhetoric and hackneyed gesture—with greater boldness:

> It is Lincoln pardoning the fellow who slept on sentry duty. It is the grace of the Bixby letter. The least private would find a woman to caress him, a woman in an old shawl—with a great bearded face and a towering black hat above it, to give unearthly reality.

Since the writing of Walt Whitman's elegy, *When Lilacs Last in the Dooryard Bloom'd,* Dr. Williams is, I think, the first American to give the huge, unwieldy myth of

Lincoln a new and vivid semblance of reality. A literal reading of Dr. Williams's image is, of course, the false one, and the pit of history waits for those unhappy creatures who attempt it.

If, as I believe, *In the American Grain* contained the proofs of a living heritage in American prose some fifteen years ago, it should be said again that it seems even more alive today. And unless I am very much mistaken, that quality of freshness which few poems and fewer works of prose possess will endure within it for many years to come.

ON A VISIT TO LONDON'S NATIONAL
PORTRAIT GALLERY IN 1934

THE National Portrait Gallery looks like a bank, a square, graystone, sturdy annex to the more imposing façade of the National Gallery. Its foundations seem rooted in rock and iron under Trafalgar Square; it is permanent and safe, a good place to lock up valuables, standing withdrawn, yet in full sight of Nelson's monument and it is just around the corner from the quick tide of traffic that circles Piccadilly. Perhaps it is actually a bank, and its tall chambers are safety vaults to house the dead, the famous dead in their familiar attitudes of life. The Gallery, then, is rather less a gallery than a compromise between a public library and a national churchyard where one may trace the origin of the million faces seen on the streets of London, faces at noon at Waterloo Station, in Soho, the Thames Embankment, or down the Strand.

One looks for history here and not for art; and the atmosphere, like so much (too much) of English painting, is literary. Pay your sixpence, walk up the stairs; the way is broad and the halls are empty. As one enters a wide reception-hall, members of the present royal family and a wide semi-circle of diplomats in World War treaty conferences are quickly passed by. These figures, spread on canvas and framed in heavy gilt, are wooden creatures, and are far less lively than our memory of them in the feature sections of illustrated newspapers. Strangely enough, history begins with an American by an American—the Sargent portrait of Henry James.

Somehow the reproductions of this familiar head, shoulders, and upper torso have never done the original canvas justice. Seeing him here, quite as Sargent left him, James seems to dominate the room, and, for a moment, seems more English than his peers. His head is John Bull's head—round and full-blooded, bald—and was this why the Suffragists slashed at the canvas? They were in a hurry to get things done and slashed in fury, but, had they looked longer, they would have discerned a gaze of defiance, most un-English, in the candid eyes that met their own. They would have seen that the left thumb, hooked into the armhole of the vest, showed an aggressiveness beyond mere male complacency after a Sunday dinner. In this gesture he betrays that moment of boldness which comes to every timid man and he seems determined, despite long sentences and longer fits of shyness, to be heard at last and honored in a foreign land. One almost hears the hesitant, persistently low voice echoing across drawing rooms where James imagined himself unwanted, and in spite of silences which cleared his way, ignored. Pale Sir Edmund Gosse, beside him on the wall, is infinitely more assured than he, for Sir Edmund could well afford a show of modesty, and could peer nearsightedly into the faces of many friends at tea, friends who brought him praise and fame and offered him posts of authority on lecture platforms and in literary weeklies.

Across the room from Gosse and James is a young woman who would remain unrecognized were it not that her name appears in brass below the portrait. She is Marian Evans and this likeness of her was painted, I would say, before "George Eliot" gave her a weighty reputation. Here she has sunlit yellow hair and a red-rose and white complexion. The heavy features that we know so well, the half-closed eyes and heavy lips, the face that seems to be the proper image of her who wrote in semiclassic beef-and-pudding prose, are of a later sitting. Perhaps the signs of heaviness are here, but they can be mistaken for robust health and pre-maternal animal calmness, as yet untouched by years of hard-won dignity and the lack of a fixed social position in society. The face that smiles down at us seems now reflected in the faces of the lower middle classes. These very features, sharpened slightly and less smiling, are to be found in the faces of barmaids and ribbon clerks, and those women who are stationed behind glass cages in restaurants and hotels. These, like the face above us, seem preternaturally calm, yet they retain their calmness with a grim edge of resistance to the memory of Victorian womanhood. They tower over the little men surrounding them and stand guard over fleets of deferential bell boys and suave waiters. Efficient management is in the air, and through each swift action British serenity (so it seems) must be maintained.

George Eliot, however, is not the only woman in the room. Here are the Brontë sisters, and, among others, a certain mother and daughter who effect a singular contrast in personality. Of course, the two are Mary Wollstonecraft and Mary Shelley, and, if the mother has an obvious advantage, some credit must be given to John Opie, her portrait painter. Human warmth entered each canvas as he touched it with his brush, and the woman before him was a nearly perfect model for his talent. He did not, however, invent the rich lips and generous mouth, nor the warm light that radiated from her body. It was she who transmuted something of her own warmth to the chilly blood of William Godwin; and it was she who changed him, as though by some chemic miracle, into a lover. His humanitarianism was of the kind that fed itself upon abstractions; whatever emotions he possessed were quick to die and found their substitute in silent anger and martyred pride. Her death gave him the solace of human grief, yet after it, there was nothing left but the spiritless desire to gain an income from the inheritance of his wealthy son-in-law.

It would be easy to dismiss the pretentious portrait of Mary Shelley as so much vanity and outmoded affectation. The thin lips are curved into a simper that is the worst of all possible substitutes for a smile. It is obvious that Mary Shelley was acting the part of a grand lady seated at a writing table: the red curtain behind her, the fashionable black dress, the writing implements in ordered disarray about her, were details chosen for posterity to admire. The table reminds us that she was a novelist in her own right as well as the widow of a famous poet, but the rich, heavy furniture and the smart dress also remind us that she was the mother of a son who was to inherit a baronet's title and a respectable fortune.

The grand lady was not too vain, nor was she affected without good reason. In the past she had learned to fear gossip and ill fame, and she knew well, I think, that outward appearances too often fix the world's opinion of a woman. Perhaps she had a premonition that the pose struck by the grand lady in the portrait would gain respect in the Victorian age that was to follow hers. She had, moreover, the task of making her dead husband's poetry seem more suitable to the title that her son would bear, and perhaps, if such were possible, less obscure. She used what means she could to build a posthumous reputation for the poetry that had not yet found its widest audience, and, I think, it is not too much to say that the portrait is among the unconscious contributions to that end. At last she had won security and now would not relinquish it; something of that deliberate coolness that guided her father's elaborate but unsuccessful plans toward making a livelihood ran in her blood and she was not to fail.

Now that a hundred years have left Haydon's tragedy behind us, it is no longer necessary to apologize for the fantastic discrepancy between his finished work and its intention. It is enough to say that no man ever paid a higher price for being what Haydon was—a painter with a "literary" imagination; yet his portrait of Wordsworth is more convincing than all other attempts to paint the poet, and the original canvas is far more effective than any of its reproductions. The experience of seeing it on a wall is not unlike that of meeting Sargent's Henry James. Haydon, I think, loved Wordsworth with a pure heart; and by that I mean that both men met for a brief moment on common ground. Both shared a sense of awe concerning the importance of their work, their duty to themselves, their art, their nation, and the world.

Haydon's Wordsworth stands with dark mountain clouds behind him. The head and shoulders of the gaunt figure are bent forward in heavy reverie. The eyes gaze downward on a distant earth below, and under the hawk-like nose the left side of a distorted lip is suddenly revealed. This revelation of the twisted lip is a surprise, for here one sees, or rather feels, an element of deep self-pity that was to counterbalance its discontent by the sonorous music of —shall we call it—"epic pantheism"? Even the sonnets of the later Wordsworth contain an "epic" quality; the simple world of mountains, hills, and trees grown very large; and it is still the largest world that England ever knew.

This vision of a large world, so a friend has told me, is a rare experience in English art. Milton shared it and Byron embellished his possession of it in the ironic cantos of *Don Juan*. Both Blake and Shelley held outlines of this vision in the mind's eye, yet neither lived to see the edifice completed. And Hardy in his great Victorian ruin, *The Dynasts*, again looked upward and saw its rounded hemispheres. And it is not too much to say that the same vision haunted D. H. Lawrence, and in his painting the grand manner revealed itself once more. Perhaps the sight of a like vision led to Haydon's suicide. He could not guide his hand to encompass that thing he valued most, but as he saw its semblance rise in Wordsworth he sketched a detail and preserved it for posterity.

Here, in this room, set in glass cases on a center table, rest the life masks of Keats and Blake. Keats is the prototype of the "little" Londoner one sees on the less-crowded thoroughfares; the sensitive lips, the delicately veined eyelids, are of the type. But these whom we meet now have no release in words for the sensibilities that are revealed in a graceful inflection of the voice or in a final gesture of the hand. They stand at bookstalls in Bloomsbury or wander, black-hatted, through Soho Square. They are to be found under the shelter of a German bookshop near Charing Cross and some admit a recent conversion to Communism. But it is the type that we rediscover, and not the poet, for the poets of England's twentieth century wear other masks with which to face the world.

Contrast to Keats lies in the head of Blake; here is the compact jaw, and the full lips set in a straight line, as though the muscles of the face were controlled by some centrifugal force. Here one may well imagine a tenacity of purpose seldom discovered in those erratic flashes of genius which illuminate his poetry. The face is a self-righteous face which is the moral aspect of true heresy; by gazing inward he saw that godlike image of his own strength, but the effort demanded more than human effort could sustain, and his prophetic books, if one regards them as works of art, remain still-born.

After a circuit of the many faces in this room, a circuit extending backward from the end of the nineteenth century to its beginning, one says good-by by stopping for a moment at the large, dark portrait of Leigh Hunt. There is no denying the man's charm, nor the attraction of the intelligent brown eyes with their quick appeal to human sympathy. It would be difficult to refuse him anything, or to remember that he had once borrowed money from you. Many of his friends could testify to his liberal service in their cause. His praise of their poetry came from his lips as easily as most men breathed the fragrance of spring air. The benevolent quickness in his eyes made praise such as his a special gift, a gift to be offered and accepted without embarrassment. In return he asked the right to live, to smile as he smiles here, dependent on your good humor, your purse, your willingness to respond with human tolerance to human weakness.

Upstairs, the eighteenth century revives itself again. The more or less predictable knowledge of the world's affairs is written large in the faces that Sir Joshua Reynolds knew so well, and in them we see again those signs of maturity that the nineteenth century discloses in the features of its scientists alone: Faraday, Owen, Huxley, Darwin. We have learned rather too well the eighteenth century attitude of elegance, its love of fine linen and brocaded velvets. And because of this we are not prepared to see the restlessness that animates the room: Matt Prior looking up from his busy writing table as though about to speak; Bonnie Prince Charlie, as a boy, breathless, as though he had run into the room and were about to leave again at once; Laurence Sterne sitting on the edge of a chair, forcing a heavy white-lipped smile in a brief interview. Despite their courtesy, despite a background which reveals a succession of calm Georgian interiors, there is something almost American in their demand for movement. Tobias Smollett, with his red nose and shrewd blue eyes, seems about to ask a question and turn away, and there, of course, is a theatrical portrait of David Garrick, trying his best to represent tragedy, melodrama, comedy, and farce with both eyes wide and staring into nowhere. This is not (as one might suppose, seeing each reproduction of a canvas separately) a quiet room, for the entire company seems to move in a dozen swirls and eddies. We are mistaken, I think, if we consider the prose of the *Spectator* or the verse of Pope's *Epistles* as living apart from the conversation that was overheard at coffeehouses and at card tables.

Speaking of conversation and its entry into literature, one thinks of Boswell's famous *Life*, and from this memory of it we turn to Reynolds's excellent portrait of the early Johnson.

The early Johnson is by no means a young man; he is on the nether side of middle age, retaining, with characteristic tenacity, the vigor of forty-five. The coarse-grained skin is pale and its pallor is accentuated by the dark background that Reynolds chose for this three-quarter profile of his friend. Again one does not ask too much of "art" in the National Portrait Gallery, but I suspect that the portrait is among the best of Reynolds's work. The profile is very like a cameo or medallion, and certainly in its clear outline of forehead, nose, lips, chin, and naked throat it resembles the classic head on a Roman coin. And to this outline Reynolds had added his peculiar gift of scientific observation; with admirable candor he has painted in the nearsighted eye narrowing to a painful squint—the face is almost blind. The physical handicap is balanced against the strength of the broad neck, which is re-enforced by the dignity of the strong curving line extending down from upper forehead to the open shirt front below the throat.

As we walk upward, leaving the eighteenth century behind us in a lower gallery, the circle of English life grows smaller, and we are facing, more often than not, effigies of men and women whose activity, hopes, ambitions, began and ended in a life at court. Here is the court life of the Stuarts, and beyond them are found glimpses of the Tudors. History and legend have done well by them and they belong at this distant date to the mythology of a deeply nourished tradition. It is well to note the mixture of strength and kindliness in Cromwell's features, and amusing to recognize family resemblance to Charles the Second in the faces of the children embraced by his court ladies. But as we leave the room, we are reminded that the London street below us has little kinship to the intimacies of a life long vanished from the chambers of Old Whitehall. Nor does the skill of a Van Dyck revive those passions for which men died in a lost cause.

As we descend the stairs, the halls of the square building seem more deserted than before. The portraits seem to lock themselves within their separate chambers, and again, as one steps out to sunshine and Piccadilly, the impression of leaving a huge safety vault returns. The faces in the street, however, seem less strange, and, if your road homeward is lost, someone with Dr. Johnson's courteous compassion in his voice will point the way.

ON VIRGINIA WOOLF AND HER APPEAL TO
THE COMMON READER

IN reading Virginia Woolf at her very best—which includes *Mrs. Dalloway*, *To the Lighthouse*, *The Waves* and certain of her essays in her two *Common Readers* as well as in the present volume—it is necessary to dust off and repolish that tarnished, dented, much abused word that has become an article of kitchenware in criticism. The word is "genius." It is necessary, I believe, to say that genius, for better or for worse, means that the writer whose gifts have earned the once-coveted and shining title is the spirit of a particular time and place, a tutelar deity whose radiance sheds an unflickering, beneficent light within temple walls. Mrs. Woolf's gifts, however else we may define them, were of that quality; their residence was Bloomsbury in London and not too far from the dark and yet Alexandrian outlines of the British Museum; the moment which they suffused with pallid and clear illumination on library walls or in guest bedrooms of a country house on holidays or at eight o'clock dinner parties in the city was of the period that we now recall as existing precariously between two major wars. It was that time and place through which Mrs. Woolf's spirit moved and to which the spirit brought its endowments of sensibility and grace.

Mrs. Woolf's American publishers have thoughtfully issued E. M. Forster's tributary lecture on Virginia Woolf to accompany the posthumous collection of her essays, *The*

Death of the Moth,* a volume, by the way, which might well have been published as a third series of confidences to her *Common Reader*. Mr. Forster's tribute,† delivered in the Senate House at Cambridge on May 28, 1941, is of a sort that only he could have spoken, for the author of *Abinger's Harvest* and *A Passage to India* is another branch of the same tree which Henry James had planted in London soil and whose roots were the source of nourishment for the gifts of Dorothy Richardson as well as his own and those of Virginia Woolf. His remarks are of more penetrating eloquence than her notations on his novels in the present collection of her essays, but he has, we reflect, the advantage of the last word. As she inquires, somewhat impatiently, of Mr. Forster's work, "What next?" he proceeds calmly to celebrate the pervading charms of her personality, its freedom within the limitations she imposed, its unexpected turns of laughter, its sudden responsiveness— and despite its air of seeming guardedly aloof—before an audience of women, its virtues as a "lady" who lived upon her income of five hundred pounds a year, for she could not pretend that her mother turned a mangle, and she herself, unlike Mrs. Giles of Durham, "had never stood at the washtub." Those of us who have read Mrs. Woolf's *A Room of One's Own* would find it difficult, I think, not to recognize the personality that Mr. Forster breathes to life in an hour's lecture, and that same personality resumes its character in an essay on "Middlebrow" which Mrs. Woolf's husband saw fit to include in *The Death of the Moth;* nor does one quarrel with Mr. Forster's carefully, adroitly balanced peroration in which he says "she gave

* *The Death of the Moth*, by Virginia Woolf, 248 pp. New York: Harcourt, Brace & Co., \$3.

† *Virginia Woolf*, by E. M. Forster, 40 pp. New York: Harcourt, Brace & Co., \$1.

acute pleasure in new ways, she pushed the light of the English language a little farther against darkness."

Whatever Mr. Forster says in his brief talk reflects the sensibility of an elder inhabitant of Virginia Woolf's world as well as one who traveled beyond its sphere; so far we may be assured of his wisdom and his poise, and he has said more within the hour and some thirty-seven small, wide-margined pages than many another solemn-eyed essayist could say in a hundred large sheets of fine, closely printed type. But for my part, I find myself thinking less of Virginia Woolf as a "lady" and as a "woman," than as a daughter of Sir Leslie Stephen, the slightly ink-stained figure who in her youth was surrounded by gentlemen of late-Victorian celebrity; one thinks of Meredith, of Ruskin, of the American Ambassador, James Russell Lowell, of Robert Louis Stevenson, and, of course, Sir Edmund Gosse; one thinks of books lining the walls of a capacious library, and with them the names of writers who reappear in the pages of Mrs. Woolf's novels and essays: Sir Walter Scott, Keats, Shelley, Coleridge, Shakespeare, Horace Walpole, Edward Gibbon—but the list would grow tedious and seem inexhaustible. One begins to wonder if, after all, after writing *A Room of One's Own* and *To the Lighthouse*, she had made an escape from Sir Leslie's house and the gentlemen who came for tea? She believed she did, and there is written evidence of an exit left behind her, but a door remains open, and still one wonders, if she did escape, how far?

Far enough, one says at first, to discover a singular melody for her own prose, and Mr. Leonard Woolf, in editing this latest of her posthumous volumes, remarks upon her care in rewriting and revising the merest reviews sent off to the London *Times* Literary Supplement and the *New Statesman*. That melody, one may trust, was her great concern, and it sounded as she rehearsed and played it with the noise and chiming of many little bells.

Sometimes 'the bells rang sharply and clearly, striking their notes of nearly absolute finality in the newly published pieces on Horace Walpole, Sara Coleridge, and *Street Haunting*, but on occasion—and it is usually an occasion when the subject of the piece happens to be a romantic poet, Coleridge, or Shelley, or a Shakespearean play—the little bells ring so persistently that they seem to cover something left unsaid. Are these the moments when the escape from Sir Leslie's threshold was incomplete? When the open door behind her made it imperative that she remember Coleridge and Shelley? And because she must remember, therefore the bells chimed insistently, over and over with not too much to say?

Whether or not these questions can be answered with the directness that one might desire, it is plain enough that with few exceptions Mrs. Woolf is at her happiest as she recaptures a moment of the eighteenth century viewed always in the light of her own day. As one reads her interpretations of Walpole and Cole, of *The Historian and "The Gibbon,"* her escape seems certain; and in *Street Haunting: A London Adventure* her spirit resumes its character of genius. We are certain also that in the generation between two wars it was she who revived the so-called "familiar essay" which began its life in the formal prose of Addison, which reappeared, or rather culminated one period of its existence, in Charles Lamb's *Elia*, and then breathed fitfully until Max Beerbohm arrived in London. It is that heritage which one rediscovers in *The Death of the Moth*, and it seems natural, even in a literary sense, for Mrs. Woolf to have selected the eighteenth century as one point of its origin, a birthplace, perhaps, of her identity. The sensibility which she expressed to the admiration of her contemporaries had its likeness in the Age of Sensibility itself.

In her essays she was a mistress of what often has been called an "outmoded" form, and if one admits that the familiar essay was among the vehicles of her genius, one need not concern one's self too deeply over the question of her ability in literary criticism. She was not, I believe, vastly disturbed by problems of the intellect, and because she was not, one may find one of several reasons for her lack of ease in the presence of Coleridge. She exerted an influence in literary matters because of her gifts and her intelligence, and because her artistry embraced the arts of persuasion and of charm. It is only when her criticism appears to be incidental to the portrait of a literary figure that it becomes convincing to the eye, and when the portrait is lacking, and when the criticism takes the form of a set argument, the illumination fades, and we hear only the ringing of her small bells.

It may seem strange that her essays on Henry James, George Moore, and E. M. Forster are less good than the others, and that her *Letter to a Young Poet* offers no more than what Polonius would say. The question of her escape from what was once Sir Leslie Stephen's threshold and the distance between it and her room in Bloomsbury returns in a slightly different guise. She seems to be reminded, half-unwillingly, of her duties to the many books piled high against the wall, of her obligation to the names of Chaucer, Shakespeare, Tennyson, Keats, Byron, of upholding among her contemporaries, both young and old, a judgment that weights the page with its list of names. The names, as we know, perhaps too well, are familiars of discourse on literary subjects, but as she uses them to stress the failures of contemporary literature, they remain mere counters of discussion. In these papers one feels that she is not the fortunate genius who writes with such brilliancy of Coleridge's daughter, Sara—and the question is: Has her genius found itself again because it was spoken in the voices of two daughters of famous men, one the daughter of a poet and philosopher, the other the daughter of a knighted literary critic?

In closing this third volume of Virginia Woolf's addresses to her *Common Reader* one is impelled to say that no reading of her best work can be called complete without a knowledge of it, without the delight of hearing her genius speak again. And in her essay that recreates the magic of walking city streets at evening, "street haunting" as she called it, written in 1930, one finds a premonition of her own death, and her true epitaph:

The sights we see and the sounds we hear now have none of the quality of the past, nor have we any share in the serenity of the person who, six months ago, stood precisely where we stand now. His is the happiness of death; ours the insecurity of life. He has no future; the future is even now invading our peace. It is only when we look at the past and take from it the element of uncertainty that we can enjoy perfect peace.

ON PAUL ELMER MORE AND HIS *SHELBURNE ESSAYS*

The adventurous soul who today against reigning scientific and pragmatic dogma would maintain no vague and equally one-sided idealism, but the true duality of the one and the many, the absolute and the relative, the permanent and the mutable, will find himself subjected to an intellectual isolation and contempt almost as terrible as the penalties of the inquisition, and quite as effective in producing a silent conformity.

—*Shelburne Essays*, Seventh Series, 1910.

READING these lines some thirty years later, and almost a decade after his death in 1937, and despite his own doubts in the merits of prophecy, it would seem that Paul Elmer More had foretold the fate of his posthumous reputation. His *Shelburne Essays* have dropped out of print, and while the mention of his name reawakens echoes of respect, it recalls, not without embarrassment, the more persistent echoes of a literary quarrel which created unhappy diversions in academic circles a quarter of a century ago. In speaking of Paul Elmer More and his *Shelburne Essays*, it is not my intention to revive the heat of a Neo-Humanist controversy which flourished with such a violent show of ill-feeling that its moral issues were lost in the general confusion surrounding them. It was then agreed that Irving Babbitt, who was More's associate and friend, was the better controversialist, and that his personality with its abrasive force struck fire at more frequent intervals. It was true enough that Babbitt secured the greater number of converts to the Neo-Humanist cause; his zeal was no less than the zeal of an evangelist, and though its sincerity and high seriousness remain unquestioned, the evangelical temper which inspired the pages of his *Rousseau and Romanticism* was too obviously ill-suited to the doctrines of restraint and sanity that he essayed to preach. The decorous lamb of Neo-Humanism appeared upon the scene clothed as a lion, but its disguise which had been so artlessly assumed failed to deceive its ingenious and infinitely more worldly enemies; it was quickly stripped of the garments it had worn with such innocent and unlamblike pride, and was subsequently sacrificed on the altars of literary journalism.

Irving Babbitt's best writings are, of course, non-controversial—and it would seem an impertinence to defend his essays on the masters of French criticism or his introduction to an English version of *The Dhammapada*. The same may be said of More's *Shelburne Essays*, and it is not my purpose to defend them against an unseen attack, and at a distance of nearly forty years. They have weathered well, if somewhat obscurely, on library shelves, and a renewed acquaintance with them readily dispels the darker clouds of a half-forgotten Neo-Humanist controversy.

II

It can never be said that More underestimated the powers that he felt were ranged against his point of view, but he saw the prospect of "intellectual isolation and contempt" in almost the same spirit as one who secretly enjoys the prospect of an early martyrdom. We may admire the courage of his stand, but I cannot help but think that his invitation to an "adventurous soul" enjoined his readers to share in the disfavors of defeat, and, if so, he opened an unhappy prospect for the general furtherance of his views. Even with the rewards of an inner serenity in sight, the probability of failure was far too great—and in the very decade in which the *Shelburne Essays* were written, the hopeful first decade of the twentieth century, American life was almost totally preoccupied with the visionary as well as material aspects of success: success in extending the ranges of popular education, success in achieving the practical results of Thomas Alva Edison's researches in his laboratory, success in being admitted to New York's 400, success in being presented at the Court of St. James, success in the distribution of novels until they became "bestsellers," success in business, success in building the Panama Canal, and success in American affairs abroad—the success of John Hay's "Open Door" policy in China and President Theodore Roosevelt's successful mediation of the Russo-Japanese War. Against all this, More's invitation seemed more austere than it does today; and it seemed more bleak and less certain of achieving a distant victory than a contemplation of the darkest of Thorstein Veblen's gloomy prophecies. It was not that More's views of the future were too black, but that they held the colorless vistas of white and gray. I may be speaking here of a superficial aspect of More's work, but it is one that is almost certain to catch the eye of an impressionable reader:

I cannot doubt [he wrote in the third series of his *Shelburne Essays*] that there are some in the world today who look back over the long past and watch the toiling of the human race toward peace as a traveller in the Alps may with a telescope follow the mountain-climbers in their slow ascent through the snows of Mont Blanc; or again they watch our labours and painstaking in the valley of the senses and wonder at our grotesque industry; or look upon the striving of men

196

to build a city for the soul amid the uncertainties of this life, as men look at the play of children who build castles and domes in the sands of the seashore and cry out when the advancing waves wash all their hopes away.

If one accepts this as a perspective through which More saw the world, the image of Mont Blanc rises to command a view below it, and at that distance, beyond the intimate noises of beach and shore, and where the cry of a human voice, if heard at all, sounds thin and shrill, one sees a wave advance—is it white or gray?—to wash away the castles in the sand.

It is at this distance, and when he is not at his best, that More sometimes fails to meet the moral issues he discerns; they seem remote, or hypothetical, or merely "literary" in the bad sense of the term, and it is as though More had seen them from the steps of the Widener Library at Harvard or from the windows at Bryn Mawr. Throughout his essays one traces the marks of European travel, yet the paths skirt the great cities of London, Paris, and Berlin in favor of the tourist routes of Switzerland and Italy. The paths were those of an academician's holiday from which he viewed "the unshadowed splendour of Mont Blanc" in a little room with a Tauchnitz Edition of Byron's *Don Juan* in his hand. At these moments the setting always seems as though it were a shade too pleasantly suburban; even in his retreat to Shelburne's rural beauties, there to enjoy a rediscovery of Thoreau's Walden in the congenial surroundings of brooks and birds and forest greenery, the atmosphere was very nearly as suburban as many sections of New England are today. For since the turn of the old century into the present, New Hampshire has been the summer residence of the well-to-do from Cambridge and from Boston.

In a sense (and by this I do not mean that life in an American university or college is an "escape from life") academic surroundings seem to promote a slightly suburban air. In America the physical aspects of our centers of learning tend to resemble the country club, and, truly enough, many of its vital social activities are concentrated in undergraduate supper clubs and fraternities that however discouraged re-emerge under new names on the campus. By the very nature of the task that it performs, an educational institution does not present the hardiest alternatives for a moral critic of American life; its realities are such that they seem unworldly to the man of affairs. Its true limitations have been seriously discussed by Henry Adams, who did not go so far as to say with John Jay Chapman "that teaching dethrones the intellect," but wrote his *Education* for everyone to read; and the limitations are sufficient to explain why no great novel, no first-rate play, nor even a document comparable to Saint-Simon's memoirs of the court of Louis XIV can come to life within them.

We may be grateful, I think, that another moral critic of literature, Samuel Johnson, so dismally failed in his teaching a boys' grammar school at Litchfield that he took the road with David Garrick, his ex-pupil, to seek his fortune at his nation's capital. How deeply Johnson loved his London is well known, but his love was not inspired nor enhanced by the fact that London was an easy place for him in which to live. We know that it was not; and by the time that Boswell met him, the poise that he had achieved was at the cost of knowing profoundly the wells of human suffering around him and of tasting their depths reflected in his own soul. At each turn of his career his gifts were tested by conflict or agreement with the best minds of his age. In this respect few moral critics (and More was not

198

among them) have suffered or enjoyed Johnson's particular advantages—and what we value most in Johnson's writings, even in his notes on Shakespeare, is the distinctly unliterary character of his observations. In his notes on Falstaff we find the following comment and we delight in the sharpness and depth of his psychological insight:

Every man who feels in himself the pain of deformity, however, like this merry knight, he may affect to make sport with it among those whom it is his interest to please, is ready to revenge any hint of contempt upon one whom he can use with freedom.

We may feel that in some few of his literary judgments Johnson is steadfastly, and at times, cheerfully wrong. We know the limitations that were imposed by the formidable army of his prejudices, which included a dislike of Fielding and a distrust of Scotsmen and Americans, yet within the world he knew so well (and that world was at his nation's heart and was circumscribed by one of the great cities of modern civilization) the rightness of judgment remains as sound as on the day he wrote his note on one of King Henry's speeches:

Shakespeare urges this aggravation of the guilt of treachery with great judgment. One of the worst consequences of breach of trust is the diminution of that confidence which makes the happiness of life, and the dissemination of suspicion, which is the poison of society.

We cannot expect to find anything of like derivation in Paul Elmer More's *Shelburne Essays*, and turning westward from Johnson's London, we enter a more rarefied, brighter, harsher, and (if I may say so, even in praise of America's most distinguished Humanist) a less distinctly humanized atmosphere.

III

Someone has spoken—it does not matter who, for no doubt many others have made the same observation—of the delightful urbanity of the prose which graces the early *Shelburne Essays*. Urbanity in prose was one of the standards by which the nineteenth century measured its approval of an essay in literary criticism, and an early twentieth-century reaction against the arts of being urbane was natural; urbanity seemed to cover a lack of seriousness, to remind one, if ever so slightly, of the hypocritical heart that knew of neither Freud nor Jung, and yet was satisfied to beat its tatoo securely beneath a tightly buttoned-up frock-coat. In rereading the *Shelburne Essays* we are aware of their proximity to the Victorian scene in literature, and More could not deny his affection for its lesser figures, its Lionel Johnson, its George Gissing, or a forgotten poetess, Louisa Shore, but however urbane he may have seemed, there is no lack of seriousness in what he had to say. And today, now that the nineteenth century is at a proper distance behind us, we are less frightened by the presence of its urbanity than we were, let us say, twenty-five years ago. To speak of Tennyson or of Longfellow no longer awakens the discomfort that was once felt. We are in a position to see how steadily More viewed the merits and flaws of Longfellow's poetry, how careful he was not to patronize it, or to dismiss its hold upon popular imagination. In reading his essay on Longfellow, one discerns More's mingled debt to an Emersonian habit of speech and his affection for that most urbane of nineteenth century essayists, Charles Lamb. One sees and hears that heritage throughout the essay, and its eloquence is clearly overheard in the concluding paragraph in which More speaks of Longfellow's adaptations from Dante:

We need have no fear of paying homage to a poet who wrote such lines as these. And he himself, if he did not, like Dante and his peers, build at the great cathedral of song, did at least add to it a fair and homely chapel, where also, to one who comes humbly and reverently, the eternal ages watch and wait.

Perhaps the flourish at the end of his last sentence is still a shade too rhetorical for our taste, but it was said gracefully, and after More had stated plainly that Longfellow's great weakness was in mistaking the offices of fancy for those of imagination. No critic in America has written of Longfellow so searchingly and well, and it is to More's enduring credit that he performed a skillful operation without maiming or disfiguring his patient—and the result (which is something extremely rare in criticism) is that after More has weighed the balance of Longfellow's tarnish and brass against his merits, one returns to a reading of his poetry with a keener, if more strictly limited, appreciation than before.

In his *Shelburne Essays*, More practiced the art of suspending his esthetic and moral judgments, and one awaits, quite as one waits for the fall of an ax, for the place and the moment at which the sharpened edges of his discrimination are going to fall. More's temperament was far too seriously inclined to allow for a play of wit, and on the rare occasions when he did employ it, it arrives with the sensation of an overweighted shock upon the sensibilities of the reader. Something of that shock is felt as one reads his comment on Arthur Symons's verse:

There are things it were good for a man, even for a decadent poet, not to have written, and these poems to Bianca, with their tortuous effort to find the soul in the ambiguities and unclean curiosities of a swaying will are of them. They are a waste of shame.

Since we are on the subject of More's remarks concerning the "decadence" or Symbolism of Mr. Symons's poetry I think a word should be said of More's general attitude toward Symbolism. As he wrote of Mr. Symons's "unclean curiosities," which does seem strong language to apply as one rereads a stanza or two of flaccid and derivative verse, More's position was by no means untenable. The verse is weak and one is not disposed to defend it, but when one comes across More's remark that Baudelaire's poetry is equally "unclean," a warning is sounded that we should not ignore. The same warning is heard as we reread More's attempts to elevate the talents of Lionel Johnson and Lady Augusta Gregory above the poetic gifts of W. B. Yeats. It is not enough to say that More's moral philosophy demanded a consistency that would automatically reject Yeats's poetry and the presence of Baudelaire; that consistency had already suffered a compromise in More's acceptance of Dante Gabriel Rossetti's poetry and James Thomson's poem, *The City of Dreadful Night*. In respect to Baudelaire and Yeats, More's rejection of their poetry has two slightly different faces than the one he presents to Romantic "decadence" in British verse. His language is that of nineteenth century criticism, and nineteenth century criticism was not equipped to recognize the techniques in poetry that the early Symbolists employed and passed on to their heirs. Another aspect of More's rejection of Yeats and Baudelaire is more closely related to the thoroughly Protestant character of his morality, and he was always likely to seem capricious or uncertain whenever he spoke of an Irish literature or entered the presence of what Henry Adams discerned at Mont-Saint-Michel and Chartres.

In both word and spirit, More had seen "decadence"

at work in a literature that started bravely enough with the Lake Poets, and declined through the course of a century to the less happy moments of Mrs. Browning, Swinburne, and William Morris, and there is no need for me to re-enlarge upon that kind of "decadence" here. Yet what of the Symbolists and their heritage which has affected every major poet who came early or late to his maturity between 1900 and the beginning of the second World War? We should admit that where More saw merely a continuation of the "decadence" that he perceived so clearly in the doctrines, the verse, and the prose of Oscar Wilde, E. A. Robinson, More's contemporary, had been refreshed by a discovery of Verlaine, and W. B. Yeats had found a touchstone for lyrical impressionism in Mallarmé. Yet the very poets who received the greatest benefit from a youthful enthusiasm in practicing the techniques and attitudes of Symbolism, also outgrew them, or so modified the original canons of its esthetic that one cannot speak of their best poetry as stemming solely and directly from its influence. What More underestimated was the hardiness (with all its seeming frailty and lassitude) of the poetic imagination possessed by Yeats. In general, all literary movements, no matter what their names may be, fail to circumscribe the gifts of a writer who is fortunate enough to arrive at his maturity; but the less gifted are always left behind, suffering the limitations of a particular school, or the instructions of an early master.

If More saw little of the strength that was implicit in Yeats's slowly maturing genius, he was by no means uncertain of the values that Hawthorne's imagination brought to light, or the salutary results of reappraising the poetry of George Crabbe. More may have been aware (but this one cannot prove) that his perception of Crabbe's merits had been shared by E. A. Robinson; if it was not, there is still room for speculation as to whether Robinson had read his essay, either as it appeared in a periodical, or after it was gathered into a selection of a *Second Series of Shelburne Essays* in 1905. However that may be, there is a passage in More's essay on Crabbe that parallels and re-illuminates one of the major themes of Robinson's poetry. More wrote of Crabbe:

His own early life in a miserable fishing hamlet on the Suffolk coast, under a hard father, his starving years of literary apprenticeship in London, and then for a time the salt bread of dependency as private chaplain to the Duke of Rutland, acquainted him with many sorrows which years of comparative prosperity could not entirely obliterate. He is at bottom a true Calvinist, showing that peculiar form of fatalism which still finds it possible to magnify free will, and to avoid the limp surrender of determinism. Mankind as a body lies under a fatal burden of suffering and toil, because as a body men are depraved and turn from righteousness; but to the individual man there always remains open a path up from darkness into light, a way out of condemnation into serene peace. And it is with this mixture of judicial aloofness and hungering sympathy that Crabbe dwells on the sadness of long and hopeless waiting, the grief of broken love, the remorse of wasted opportunities, the burden of poverty, the solitude of failure, which run like dark threads through most of his *Tales.*

The setting of Crabbe's verse as More interpreted it recalls the atmosphere of Robinson's poem, *The Man Who Died Twice*, but more important than a general resemblance of human sympathy and insight is More's specific observation that *to the individual man there always remains open a path up from darkness into light, a way out of condemnation into serene peace.* This is what the man who died twice has to say even with his last breath:

He asked strangely, "You see that I'm content.
I shall not have to be here very long,
And there's not much that I may do for God
Except to praise him. I shall not annoy you,
Or your misguided pity, with my evangel,
For you must have yours in another dress."

And with a lighter measure of poetic tact and grace, Robinson reiterated the theme in *Archibald's Example:*

"My green hill yonder, where the sun goes down
Without a scratch, was once inhabited
By trees that injured him—an evil trash
That made a cage, and held him while he bled.

"Gone fifty years, I see them as they were
Before they fell. They were a crooked lot
To spoil my sunset, and I saw no time
In fifty years for crooked things to rot.

"Trees, yes; but not a service or a joy
To God or man, for they were thieves of light.
So down they came. Nature and I looked on,
And we were glad when they were out of sight.

"Trees are like men, sometimes; and that being so,
So much for that." He twinkled in his chair,
And looked across the clover to the place
That he remembered when the trees were there.

In his temperamental responsiveness to Crabbe's verse, More is far more persuasive than in his attack on Arthur Symons or in his praise of Mrs. Gaskell's novels; his moral earnestness which in certain of his essays seems so shrill and out of key resumes its poise as one reads what he had to say on the subject of solitude and Nathaniel Hawthorne. In this essay, and through the twentieth century's respect for Henry James (whose monograph on Nathaniel Hawthorne in the English Men of Letters series is one of the finest critical biographies in modern literature) and by a path that More felt was the "teaching . . . of the universal protest of the human heart," those limitations, which so frequently had placed him behind the invisible line marked by the first hour struck in the year of nineteen-hundred, begin to drop away. Speaking as I am from the mid-years of the century that More so heartily mistrusted, and indeed, a measure of his distrust is justified by our experiences in the presence of two World Wars, his illumination of Hawthorne's "philosophic symbolism" (the phrase is his) may seem more fashionable than More himself would have desired. To *The Solitude of Nathaniel Hawthorne* More brought those resources that he had gained in his studies of India's forest philosophers and from his well-considered knowledge of the Orestean cycle in Greek tragedy. How pertinently he wrote of Hawthorne when he said:

But if Aeschylus and Hawthorne are alike poets of Destiny and of the fateful inheritance of woe, their methods of portraying the power and handiwork of Ate are perfectly distinct. The Athenian too represents Orestes, the last inheritor of the curse, as cut off from the fellowship of mankind; but to recall the Orestean tale, with all its tragic action of murder and matricide and frenzy, is to see in a clearer light the originality of Hawthorne's conception of moral retribution in the disease of inner solitude. There is in difference something, of course, of the constant distinction between classic and modern art; but added to this is the creative idealism of Hawthorne's rare and elusive genius.

This, I believe, is one of the happiest of More's analogies, and as he speaks of Hawthorne's "rare and elusive genius,"

I doubt if there are many better examples, such as More has given us, of an artist's dual responsibility to life and art. The very theme of his essay seems to have touched a hidden spring in More's imaginative life, and the images that rise from it are those that show the subtle likenesses and contrasts between the peace of solitude and the terrors of human isolation.

It is in this vein that More wrote his essay on *Nemesis, or the Divine Envy*, in which the instruction, *Think as a mortal*, runs as an obbligato through its theme. The instruction itself is a familiar law of ethical discourse, and if restated baldly it has little meaning to the modern ear, but it was More's intention to renew its life, and as in his essay on Hawthorne's solitude, he calls on the spirit of Aeschylus to illustrate his text:

With implacable zeal the Erinyes hunt down earthly glory that vaunts itself unduly. So in the play of Aeschylus they exclaim: "The vanity of men and their pride that toucheth the sky,—all this melteth at our dark-stoled approach, it wasteth away unhonoured under earth." In these fearful daughters of Night the Greek beheld the penalty that overtakes those who forget in pride or madness to think as mortals: and woe to the man whom some higher law impels to disdain these avenging deities, whether it be a Hamlet of the modern world driven on by conscience and ghostly apparitions, or an Orestes summoned by oracular voices to confront their wrath in pursuance of a sterner duty. And woe to the man whom the gods have endowed with superhuman wisdom, for to him also the grace of heaven is not without peril.

I think I am not far wrong if I assume that the tone of these remarks is scarcely that of one who is merely an accomplished reader in comparative literatures—something else is there, and I believe it to be the voice of a man who had come to speak a sermon. The voice was heard when

Samuel Johnson wrote his *Life of Richard Savage*, and it was decidedly less agreeable to the ear of the reader twenty-five years ago than it is today. I think I am not wrong when I say that we are less frightened by More's approach to his subject than in the days of revolt against the Puritan tradition in American literature; to admit that men are less than gods does not infringe, I hope, upon those liberties which have survived the events and the emergencies of the past thirty years.

The preaching of a lay sermon is, of course, a dangerous practice for any modern writer, and his greatest danger (which may arrive as a tribute to his gifts) is to become the leader of a literary cult; it was that misfortune which attended the latter years of D. H. Lawrence's life, and within it there are many open trap-doors through which the unwary writer falls. To find and perhaps to preach sermons in stones may have done very well for the companions of the melancholy Jaques in Arden's forest, but we remember those sermons best when they were recited as conscious parodies of their devotions, and in that old play it is the clown who rules the scene.

In rereading More it is not difficult to recall that the best of Emerson's prose writings were those that could be read as though they were delivered from a pulpit, and I think there can be little doubt that it was More's intention to strengthen, even though it seemed to narrow, the vein of Humanism which runs its course throughout the somewhat amorphous, and certainly all-embracing teachings of Emerson. The failure of Emerson's idealism was one of the contributing causes of the tragic failure of Woodrow Wilson's position at the close of the first World War: could we say that in his moment of pride that Woodrow Wilson failed to think as a mortal?

There is much that might be written of More's quarrel with science in his *Shelburne Essays;* it was not a happy quarrel, and as I have said before, More was not a fortunate controversialist. His concern was that of a moral philosopher whose sensibilities responded to the "truths" that had been revealed to him through literature, and in particular, through the poetic literature of an Anglo-American tradition. Poetic "truth," of course, is of a different order than scientific "truth," and the difference between them has been best said in Mr. Basil Willey's study of *The Seventeenth Century Background:*

For in poetry thought is not pure, it is working in alliance with the feelings and the will. In Bacon's phrase, it "subjects the show of things to the desires of the mind"—which is the exact reverse of the process called science.

It is better to recognize the moral "truths" of literature as a process in reverse of a non-moral aspect of scientific thinking than to insist, as More did, that an irreconcilable quarrel existed between them. The actual "truth" that More conveys to us (and that reality is implicit in his essays on Nemesis and Hawthorne) needs no apology— but here the question is not an academic one, and is, as it should be, closely related to those ancient "truths" which are constantly refreshed and given an enduring life in poetic literature. Here, the proper relationships between man and man and gods and men are not to be denied: and is it a paradox to say that More realized the fulfillment of his moral "truths" only when he restored the practices of moral criticism to the dignity and seriousness of a fine art?

Someone has said, and with a lightness of inflection that made the statement seem disarming, that poetry itself is a moral art. And so it seems to be in the Protestant tradition

of an Anglo-American literature. The statement explains
to some degree the depths of More's perception as he regarded the values of Hawthorne's "rare and elusive genius,"
for Hawthorne, like Henry James, is among those writers
of prose whose art existed within a world of poetic realities. In his interpretations of Aeschylus and of India's forest
philosophers, Paul Elmer More shared an insight of that
world, and in his application of the precepts from ancient
sources, one rediscovers their reality in American literature.

One word more. As the present century reaches its
meridian, to be humane, and to be aware that the wrath
of Nemesis pursues the would-be conquerors of our world
acquire merits that had been forgotten before the arrival
of two World Wars. And to be humanitarian in one's
desires seems to be associated with too many of the mistakes
that we have made. The broad wave of Humanitarianism
itself seems to be slowly ebbing in its strength. It has spread
too thinly, for the trials of the present century are not
washed away by it, and there is too much evidence of
wreckage on its shores. If I may be permitted to dismiss
my metaphor and to speak plainly of a conflict between
two words that has gone on longer than anyone cares to
remember, let us say that the virtues of being humane have
more inherent strength and a deeper penetration into a true
knowledge of the human spirit than the transient rewards
of the humanitarian impulse and its facile disillusionments.
But as More once wrote, "these questions that touch man's
deepest moral experience are not capable of logical solution; indeed, they lose all reality as soon as they are subjected to dogmatic definition." The knowledge that we
truly seek is how to live, and to do so we turn with More
to those realities that the Greeks perceived in the presence
of Divine Envy and that Hawthorne saw when he wrote

his fable of *The Minister's Black Veil*. It is in these terms that the answer must be read, in the very image of Nemesis, in the tragedy of Orestes, in the story of Job's trial, and in the maturity of Adam's knowledge as he left the garden of Eden.